See the
Wider picture

The eccentric Cadillac Ranch, Amarillo, Texas, USA

Three artists built Cadillac Ranch in 1974 beside the famous Route 66.
They created the installation by half-burying 10 old Cadillacs nose
down in the ground. The cars are placed at the same angle as the face
of the Great Pyramid of Giza in Egypt. You can add your own graffiti,
but make sure you take a photo because it will soon be painted over by
someone else.

What would you paint?

Pearson Education Limited
KAO Two
KAO Park
Hockham Way
Harlow, Essex
CM17 9SR
England
and Associated Companies throughout the world.

www.pearsonenglish.com

First published 2017

ISBN: 978-1-292-17876-9

Eighteenth impression 2023

Set in Harmonica Sans
Printed in Slovakia by Neografia

Acknowledgements
The Publishers would like to thank all the teachers and students around the world who contributed to the development of Wider World, especially the teachers on the Wider World Teacher Advisory Panel:
Irina Alyapysheva, CEE; Reyna Arango, Mexico; Marisa Ariza, Spain; Ana Isabel Arnedo, Spain; Alfredo Bilopolski, Argentina; Isabel Blecua, Spain; Camilo Elcio de Souza, Brazil; Ingrith del Carmen Ríos Verdugo, Mexico; Edward Duval, Belgium; Norma González, Argentina; Natividad Gracia, Spain;Claribel Guzmán, Mexico; Izabela Lipińska, Poland; Fabián Loza, Mexico; Miguel Mozo, Spain; Huỳnh Thị Ái Nguyên, Vietnam; Joacyr Oliveira, Brazil; Montse Priego, Spain; Gladys Rodriguez, Argentina; Lyudmila Slastnova, CEE; Juan Felipe Sonda García, Mexico; Izabela Stępniewska, Poland.

Photo Acknowledgements
The Publishers would like to thank the following for their kind permission to reproduce their photographs:

(Key: b-bottom; c-centre; l-left; r-right; t-top)

123RF.com: pxhidalgo 21br, Andrew Rhodes 60br; **Alamy Images:** Ashley Cooper pics 21cl, Blend Images 47b, Sergey Borisov 28/4, Design Pics Inc 70r, Lev Dolgachov 85cl, Robert Fried 116, Hero Images Inc. 105br, Juice Images 76/1, 109br, K7335 28/5, MBI 3r, Phil Crean A 45tr, Fedor Selivanov 33br, Perov Stanislav 120, Anna Stowe 13cl, Wavebreak Media ltd 122, Westend61 GmbH 81cr; **BBC Worldwide Learning:** 40 (A), 40 (B), 40 (C), 40 (D), 52tl, 52tr, 52cl, 52cr, 52b, 112tl, 112tr, 112bl, 112br; **City Montessori School (CMS):** 106br; **Fotolia.com:** Alekss 73cr, andriigorulko 35c, 35bl, glazok 35br, kaninstudio 23cr, olyina 35bc, sergojpg 35cl, ViewApart 69br; **Getty Images:** Hero Images 76/4; **Nixie Labs, Inc.:** 9 (B); **Pearson Education Ltd:** Studio 8 2, 3tl, 4tl, 5, 8, 10, 14, 15, 20, 22, 26, 27, 32, 34, 38, 39, 44, 46, 50, 51, 56, 58, 62, 63, 68, 70tl, 74, 75, 80, 82, 86, 87, 92tl, 94, 98, 99, 104, 106tl, 110, 111, Jules Selmes 33tr, 76br; **PhotoDisc:** 6tl, 18, 30, 42l, 54tl, 66, 78, 90, 102tl; **Photostage Ltd:** 45cr, 45b; **Rex Shutterstock:** Steven Haywood www.sghaywood.com / Shutterstock 92cr; **Shutterstock. com:** 101akarca 57b, 2xSamara.com 71bl, Amble Design 28/6, Andresr 76/2, Paul Aniszewski 28/2, BlueSkyImage 12tl, 24, 36, 48, 60tl, 72, 84, 96, 108, Couperfield 93br, DenisNata 76/3, Dragon Images 13tl, 25tl, 37, 49, 61, 73tl, 85tl, 97, 109tl, egd 28/3, Igumnova Irina 28/1, Ljiljana Jankovic 25r, Yaroslav Kazakov 45c, Sergey Peterman 9tl, 21tl, 33tl, 45tl, 57tl, 69tl, 81tl, 93tl, 105tl, StockLite 11tl, 23tl, 35tl, 47tl, 59tl, 71tl, 83tl, 95tl, 107tl, Wallenrock 83b; **Sole Power LLC:** Joseph Brown 9 (C); **The Kobal Collection:** Columbia / EON / Danjaq / MGM / Olley, Jonathan 42t; **Ultimate Ears:** 9 (A)

Illustration Acknowledgements
A Corazon Abierto (Sylvie Poggio) p. 3, 16, 64, 95, 100
Tim Bradford (Illustration Web) p. 4, 102
The Boy Fitz Hammond p. 6, 23, 54, 67
John Lund (Beehive) p. 12, 79, 107
Mark Ruffle (Beehive) p. 40
Maria Serrano Canovas (Plum Pudding) p. 11, 59, 90, 94

Every effort has been made to trace the copyright holders and we apologise in advance for any unintentional omissions. We would be pleased to insert the appropriate acknowledgement in any subsequent edition of this publication.

CONTENTS

0

Activities and interests; Likes and dislikes;
Home and furniture; *There is/are* with *some/any*;
Possessive adjectives and possessive *'s*

Welcome to Woodley Bridge

VOCABULARY

Activities and interests | Home and furniture | Jobs | Clothes and accessories | Countries and languages

GRAMMAR

There is/are with *some/any* | Possessive adjectives and possessive *'s* | Present Simple with adverbs of frequency | Present Continuous | *was/were*; *there was/were* | Past Simple: regular verbs

SPEAKING

Likes and dislikes | Talking about feelings

1 Match 1–5 with a–e to make sentences.

1 [c] I don't like doing
2 [ ] We love going
3 [ ] Do you like listening
4 [ ] I don't like reading
5 [ ] My dad likes taking

a books.
b to the cinema.
c ~~nothing – it's boring!~~
d photos, especially family photos.
e to music?

2 Complete the sentences with the words below. There are two extra words.

| can can't doesn't don't likes ~~love~~ stand

1 I *love* going shopping with my friends, especially when I have money to spend.
2 Jake _____ watching films at home, but I prefer going to the cinema.
3 I can't _____ waiting for people. It really annoys me!
4 My dad _____ mind giving me money. He's really kind!
5 My brother _____ stand walking to school. He always gets the bus.

3 Write the correct home and furniture word for each definition.

1 You sit in this to wash yourself. **b a t h**
2 You lie on this to sleep. **b _ _**
3 This is made of glass, so you can see through it. **w _ _ _ _ _**
4 You eat meals in this room. **d _ _ _ _ _ _   r _ _ _**
5 You can see yourself if you look in this. **m _ _ _ _ _**

4 Choose the correct option.

1 (There's)/ *There are* a big table in the dining room.
2 *There's / There are* lots of clothes on the floor in my bedroom.
3 There are *some / any* lovely flowers in the garden.
4 There aren't *some / any* towels in the bathroom.
5 There *isn't / aren't* a mirror in the dining room.

5 Complete the second sentence so that it means the same as the first sentence. Use possessive adjectives or the possessive *'s*.

1 These shoes belong to Jack.
These are *Jack's* shoes.
2 This car belongs to my parents.
This is _____ car.
3 Does this bag belong to you?
Is this _____ bag?
4 This garden belongs to us.
This is _____ garden.
5 That jacket belongs to Laura's dad.
That is _____ jacket.

1 Look at the pictures and complete the jobs.

1 c_hef_

2 s_____

3 h_____

4 m_____

5 f_____

6 n_____

2 Order the words to make sentences.

1 usually / lunch / have / I / at one o'clock
I usually have lunch at one o'clock.

2 always / late / Martha / is

_____

3 go / I / to school / sometimes / by bus

_____

4 Sara / often / tired / is

_____

5 never / Paul / his homework / does

_____

6 cooks / dinner / my dad / usually / for the family

_____

3 Read the dialogue. Choose the correct option.

Sam: Where ¹*you live /*(*do you live*), Liam?

Liam: I ²*live / lives* in the city centre. My dad ³*work / works* in a bank.

Sam: ⁴*Do / Does* your mum have a job too?

Liam: Yes, she ⁵*do / does*. She's a teacher, but she ⁶*not work / doesn't work* every day.

Sam: ⁷*She teach / Does she teach* at your school?

Liam: No, she ⁸*doesn't / don't*, and I'm very happy about that!

4 **WORD FRIENDS** Choose the correct words to complete the sentences.

1 I usually _____ my homework after dinner.
  a have   **b** do   **c** get

2 Do you _____ a shower every morning?
  a get   **b** go   **c** have

3 When do you usually _____ your friends?
  a see   **b** get   **c** have

4 I often _____ up late at the weekend.
  a go   **b** get   **c** do

5 We always _____ dinner at eight o'clock.
  a go   **b** have   **c** get up

6 We don't _____ school on Saturday or Sunday.
  a go   **b** go at   **c** go to

1 **Look at the pictures. Order the letters below and write the words for clothes and accessories.**

~~cakjte~~   inrreags   llsabeab pac   odoieh
tcahw   T-hitsr

1 *jacket*

2 _____

3 _____

4 _____

5 _____

6 _____

2 **Complete the sentences with the Present Continuous form of the verbs in brackets.**

1 Carla *is having* (have) a shower at the moment. Can you call back in ten minutes?

2 I can't talk to you now. I _____ (do) my homework.

3 My sisters aren't here this weekend. They _____ (visit) some friends in London.

4 We _____ (not wear) school uniform today because it's Saturday!

5 Martin _____ (not play) football at the moment. He _____ (watch) TV.

6 My parents _____ (not work) today. They _____ (sit) in the garden.

3 **Read the dialogues. Choose the correct option.**

A

A: Hi, Matt. What ¹(are you doing)/ are you do?

B: ²I'm playing / I playing a computer game, but ³I don't doing / I'm not doing very well. It's really difficult.

B

A: Hi, Laura. Where's Mark? ⁴Is he / Is sleeping?

B: No, he ⁵aren't / isn't. He's ⁶watch / watching a film in his bedroom.

C

A: ⁷Are / Do you feeling better today, Cara?

B: Yes, I ⁸do / am, thanks. ⁹I feeling / I'm feeling much better.

4 **How is each person feeling? Choose the correct answers.**

It's the first day of my holiday! The weather's lovely and I want to do lots of different things.

1 a sad   ⓑ excited   c nervous

All my friends are away this weekend. It's raining outside and there's nothing to do!

2 a bored   b shocked   c excited

I don't like it when my sister wears my clothes. She never asks me first!

3 a worried   b relaxed   c irritated

I've got a Maths test tomorrow. The tests are always really difficult, so I never do very well.

4 a nervous   b tired   c relaxed

I always go to bed late, so I never get much sleep. I want to sleep now!

5 a excited   b shocked   c tired

It's Saturday morning and I haven't got any homework this weekend! I wonder what's on TV.

6 a relaxed   b frightened   c annoyed

1 Complete the sentences with words for countries and languages.

1 Jacek is from *Poland* , so he speaks Polish.

2 My cousins live in Germany, so they can speak

_____ .

3 Ana is from _____ , so she speaks Italian.

4 I want to visit China, so I'm learning to speak _____ .

5 My aunt lives in Paris, in _____ , so she can speak French.

6 Maria is from Portugal, so she speaks _____ .

7 People speak Turkish in _____ .

8 We often go on holiday to Spain, so we're learning to speak _____ .

2 Choose the correct answers.

1 _____ lots of people at the party last night – more than fifty!

   a Were   (b) There were   c There was

2 Jamie _____ at school yesterday.

   a wasn't   b were   c weren't

3 Our exams _____ very difficult last term.

   a was   b there weren't   c were

4 _____ the weather good for your holiday?

   a Were   b Was there   c Was

5 _____ many people in the restaurant last night.

   a There wasn't   b There weren't   c Weren't

6 _____ a good film on at the cinema last night?

   a Was there   b There wasn't   c Were there

3 Find the Past Simple form of the verbs in the word search. Write them next to the verbs.

W	O	R	K	E	D	S	M	P	S
E	T	R	I	E	D	T	I	C	N
D	B	F	L	C	O	O	K	E	D
R	A	B	I	A	N	P	P	I	S
L	I	K	E	D	R	P	L	L	T
I	A	A	N	R	C	E	A	I	U
V	L	K	I	T	C	D	Y	N	D
E	N	J	O	Y	E	D	E	G	I
D	E	G	B	R	R	E	D	E	E
P	L	A	N	N	E	D	E	Y	D

1 work   *worked*
2 cook   _____
3 like   _____
4 live   _____
5 try   _____
6 enjoy   _____
7 study   _____
8 play   _____
9 stop   _____
10 plan   _____

4 Complete the sentences with the Past Simple form of the verbs below.

live   ~~not enjoy~~   not play
not rain   study   want

1 I *didn't enjoy* the concert last weekend – it was terrible!

2 My parents _____ in New York when they were younger.

3 Alex _____ football yesterday because he was ill.

4 My mum _____ French at university.

5 My uncle _____ to be a pop singer when he was younger.

6 We were lucky because it _____ when we were on holiday.

5 Make questions and short answers in the Past Simple.

1 you / like / your presents? ✓

   A: *Did you like your presents?*

   B: *Yes, I did.*

2 your parents / help / you / with your homework ? ✗

   A: _____

   B: _____

3 she / invite / all her friends / to the party? ✓

   A: _____

   B: _____

4 the train / arrive / on time? ✗

   A: _____

   B: _____

6 Complete the questions with the phrases below.

how did you run   ~~what did you watch~~
when did you visit   where did Anna live
who did Karl invite   why did they play

1 *What did you watch* at the cinema last night?

2 _____ tennis in the rain?

3 _____ before she moved to London?

4 _____ to his party?

5 _____ a whole marathon?

6 _____ New York? Was it last year?

1

That's my world!

VOCABULARY
Lifestyle | Everyday technology |
Adjectives of opinion | Time

GRAMMAR
Present Simple, Present Continuous
and state verbs | Verb + -ing / verb +
to-infinitive

READING
Multiple choice

LISTENING
Listening for gist | True/False

SPEAKING
Making and responding
to suggestions

WRITING
A description

BBC CULTURE
Do smartphones make you
smarter?

I can talk about everyday technology.

1 ● Look at the pictures and complete the words.

1 t*ablet*   2 b_ _ _ _ _ _ _   3 e_ _ _ _ _ _ _

4 s_ _ _ _ _ _   5 p_ _ _ _   6 s_ _ _ _ _
                                               s_ _ _ _

7 c_ _ _ _ _   8 c_ _ _ _ _ _

2 ●● Write the correct word for each definition. Use the words in
Exercise 1.

1 It's a small, flat computer you can hold in your hands. *tablet*
2 You put this inside a camera or other piece of technology to make
   it work. _____
3 It's a piece of wire to join things together. _____
4 You use this to take a photo of yourself. _____
5 You use these to listen to music so that no one else can hear. _____
6 You push this into the wall to connect to the power supply. _____
7 You use this to put more electricity into your phone. _____
8 This is the part of a device where the sound comes out. _____

3 ● **WORD FRIENDS** Choose the correct option.

1 *go* / *make* online   4 *film* / *listen* a video
2 *send* / *listen* to music   5 *download* / *text* friends
3 *play* / *read* e-books   6 *upload* / *text* pictures

4 ●● Complete the sentences with the words below. There is one extra word.

> chat   download   games   listen   make
> messages   ~~online~~   read   send   share   text
> upload   videos

1 I usually go *online* after dinner and _____ with my friends.
2 When I find a song that I like, I _____ it and then _____ to it on my music player.
3 On holiday, I usually _____ e-books or play _____ on my tablet.
4 I use my phone to _____ my friends or send instant _____ to them.
5 I take a lot of photos, then I _____ them so I can _____ them with my friends.
6 I love music, so I watch a lot of music _____ ; I'd like to _____ a video one day!

5 ● Find eight adjectives in the word search and write them below.

A	M	A	Z	I	N	G	A	P	S
W	M	Z	A	X	G	S	I	E	N
E	B	I	F	U	N	N	Y	R	U
S	A	B	I	A	N	O	T	F	S
O	F	O	S	B	R	K	E	E	E
M	B	R	N	R	C	L	C	C	F
E	Z	I	C	O	O	L	H	T	U
F	A	N	P	W	I	H	E	X	L
D	E	G	B	R	R	E	O	E	H
A	A	E	V	N	O	I	S	Y	N

1 a*mazing*
2 f _ _ _ y
3 c _ _ l
4 n _ _ _ y
5 a _ _ _ _ _ e
6 b _ _ _ _ _ _ g
7 p _ _ _ _ _ t
8 u _ _ _ _ l

6 ● Order the letters and complete the words in the sentences.

1 What a great film! It's **b**rillian**t** (birllinta)!
2 Thank you – these flowers are l_____y (olevly)!
3 I don't want to eat this food – it's d_____g (dsigusitgn)!
4 I don't know what this is – it's very s_____e (rasntge).
5 It isn't a new phone – it's very o_____-_____d (lod-shfaioend).
6 I hate this music – it's t_____e (errtileb)!

7 ●● Choose the adjective that does NOT fit in each sentence.

1 I don't like that film. I think it's _____ .
   a terrible   (b) exciting   c boring
2 E-books are _____ because they're light and easy to carry.
   a brilliant   b perfect   c noisy
3 My old phone is _____ , but I'd like to get a new one.
   a awesome   b OK   c all right
4 Thank you for the present. What a _____ surprise!
   a nice   b disgusting   c lovely
5 I love your new tablet. It's _____ !
   a awful   b amazing   c awesome
6 I like Sara, but I don't know why she wears such _____ clothes.
   a strange   b noisy   c old-fashioned
7 He's such a _____ actor – he always makes me laugh!
   a cool   b funny   c useful

8 ●●● Complete the online profile with one word in each gap.

● ● ●

Ella Hopkins

About me

I'm really [1]*into* technology. I always have my tablet with me so I can [2]_____ online whenever I want. It's brilliant for listening [3]_____ music. I can [4]_____ songs that I like from the internet, and I've just got some new [5]_____ , so I can listen on the bus on my way to school. It's also got a really good camera. I often take photos and [6]_____ them with my friends online. I haven't got a [7]_____ stick though – I don't often take photos of myself. I send a lot of instant [8]_____ to my friends and I sometimes [9]_____ games, but not very often. My brother loves games, but he only likes really modern ones, not [10]old-_____ ones.

I can use different tenses to talk about the present.

1 ● Choose the correct option. Then mark the sentences PS (Present Simple) or PC (Present Continuous).

1 Joe's *do /(doing)* some tricks on his bike at the moment. <u>PC</u>

2 We *aren't / don't* often go to the cinema. _____

3 Sara *doesn't / isn't* wearing her helmet today. _____

4 My dad never *travels / travelling* by bus. _____

5 *Are / Do* you usually do your homework after dinner? _____

6 What *do / are* you doing here? _____

2 ● Match questions 1–6 with answers a–f.

1 | c | Are you enjoying the film?
2 | ☐ | Does your uncle live in London?
3 | ☐ | Do you go online every day?
4 | ☐ | Are they making a film?
5 | ☐ | Is Jack practising on his skateboard?
6 | ☐ | Do your friends play in a band?

a Yes, I do. I chat with friends online every evening.

b No, they aren't. They're just taking some photos.

c ~~Yes, I am. It's brilliant!~~

d Yes, they do, and they're awesome!

e No, he isn't. He's playing tennis.

f No, he doesn't. He lives in Manchester.

3 ● Complete the sentences with the Present Simple form of the verbs below.

| feel ~~know~~ not understand think want

1 I *know* Kate very well – she's my best friend.

2 I'm going home because I _____ ill.

3 I _____ what you're saying. Can you repeat it, please?

4 My brother _____ to buy a new camera.

5 I _____ she's from France, but I'm not sure.

4 ●● Complete the sentences with the Present Simple or Present Continuous form of the verbs in brackets.

1 I _____ (usually/take) photos on my phone, but today I _____ (use) my camera.

2 Jez _____ (learn) the guitar at the moment because he _____ (want) to be in a band.

3 I _____ (try) to text Anna now because I _____ (need) to speak to her.

4 We _____ (usually/cycle) to school, but it _____ (rain) today, so we _____ (go) by bus.

5 I _____ (look) for my charger. I _____ (not know) where I left it.

5 ●● Read the dialogues. Choose the correct option.

A

A: Hi. What [1]*are you doing / do you do?*

B: [2]*I try / I'm trying* to take a selfie while I'm on my skateboard, but [3]*I think / I'm thinking* it's impossible! [4]*I fall off / I'm falling off* every time I try!

B

A: [5]*Do you like / Are you liking* the new James Bond game?

B: Yes, I [6]*am / do*. But [7]*I don't spend / I'm not spending* much time on computer games at the moment because [8]*I work / I'm working* hard for my exams.

C

A: Hi! Are those your new earphones? What [9]*do you listen / are you listening* to?

B: That new band, The Feds. [10]*Do you know / Are you knowing* them?

6 ●●● Complete the email with the Present Simple or Present Continuous form of the verbs in brackets.

Hi Jack,

How are you? I [1]*'m staying* (stay) with my uncle in Birmingham this weekend because there's a big computer games show here. My uncle [2]_____ (come) to this event every year. You [3]_____ (know) I [4]_____ (love) games and I [5]_____ (play) them every day at home, so this is a great place for me. At the moment, I [6]_____ (sit) in a big hall with lots of other games fans.

We [7]_____ (try) a new game – it's awesome! I [8]_____ (wear) special earphones so I can hear all the sounds in the game really well. The only problem is it's a difficult game and I [9]_____ (not do) very well! OK, I know you [10]_____ (not like) computer games because you [11]_____ (think) they're all boring, but maybe you should try this one.

What [12]_____ (you/do) this weekend? Write and tell me.

Paul

I can find specific detail in an article and talk about unusual objects.

Gadget World
Hundreds of brilliant gadgets at amazing prices!

Read about our three top gadgets this month.

The UE Boom 2 is a small speaker with a really big sound! It's about the size of a can of drink, so you can carry it with you easily and enjoy listening to your music. It's round, so the sound comes out in all directions. It's powerful enough to fill a large room with music, so you can have a party wherever you are! It's made of strong plastic, so it's OK if you drop it and it's also waterproof, so you can use it at the beach or in the shower. And the battery lasts for fifteen hours.

Do you sometimes forget to charge your phone? Well, why not buy some EnSoles? They look like normal insoles, but they use the power that you make when you're walking to charge your phone. Just put the Ensoles in your shoes, plug your phone cable into your shoe and you can chat or text while you walk. They're really cool, and a very useful gadget.

Taking selfies is fun, but sometimes you'd like your selfie stick to be just a little bit longer. Well, the Nixie is the perfect gadget for you! It's a camera that flies! You wear it on your arm like a watch, so it's easy to carry. When you're ready to take a photo, you let it go and it flies up into the air. It knows where you are and it can follow you to take some awesome photos. It then comes back down, you catch it and put it back on your arm. Simple! The Nixie isn't available to buy yet, but you can put your name on the list to get one as soon as they're on sale.

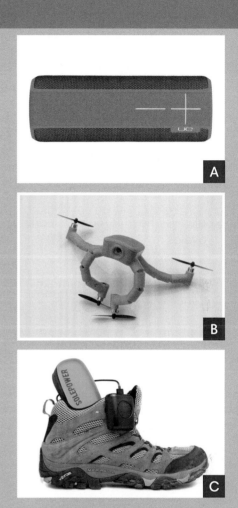

A

B

C

1 Read the text. Match gadgets 1–3 with photos A–C.

1 ☐ EnSoles 2 ☐ UE Boom 2 3 ☐ Nixie

2 Read the text again. Choose the correct answers.

1 You can only use the UE Boom 2 speaker inside a room.
   a True b False c Doesn't say
2 The UE Boom 2 speaker doesn't break easily.
   a True b False c Doesn't say
3 The EnSoles are expensive.
   a True b False c Doesn't say
4 The Ensoles use power from the sun to charge your phone.
   a True b False c Doesn't say
5 The Nixie camera is comfortable to wear.
   a True b False c Doesn't say
6 You can't buy a Nixie at the moment.
   a True b False c Doesn't say

3 Complete the sentences with the words below from the text.

| can easy lasts normal size

1 This gadget is cheap and _____ to use.
2 This camera is about the _____ of a watch, so it's very small.
3 With these earphones you _____ listen to music in the shower.
4 It looks like a _____ watch, but in fact, it's also a computer.
5 One problem with this phone is that the battery only _____ for a few hours.

I can use verb constructions with *to*-infinitives and *-ing* forms.

1 ● Order the words to make sentences.

1 enjoy / making / I / pizza
I enjoy making pizza.

2 forget / sometimes / to / do / I / my homework
_____

3 hoping / he's / pass / his exams / to
_____

4 misses / seeing / she / her cousins
_____

5 I / love / to / would / come / to the party
_____

6 always / he / his room / cleaning / avoids
_____

2 ● Match 1–6 with a–f to make sentences.

1 | c | I'm looking forward
2 | ☐ | Sonia can't
3 | ☐ | I don't
4 | ☐ | I would like
5 | ☐ | Dan is very good
6 | ☐ | Please stop

a mind helping with the party.
b making so much noise!
c ~~to seeing you.~~
d at playing the guitar.
e to go to New York.
f stand cooking.

3 ●● Complete the sentences with the correct form of the verbs in brackets.

1 My grandma is trying *to learn* (learn) how to upload pictures.

2 Why don't you come to my house when you finish _____ (do) your homework?

3 We're planning _____ (go) to France in the summer holidays.

4 Are you interested in _____ (see) the new James Bond film?

5 Mark never offers _____ (do) the washing up!

6 My sister sometimes asks me _____ (help) her with her homework.

4 ●● Find and correct the mistakes in the sentences. One sentence is correct.

1 My brother often chooses watching films on his tablet.
My brother often chooses to watch films on his tablet.

2 I can't stand to listen to that awful music!
_____

3 Hurry up – I hate being late!
_____

4 I hope my dad agrees paying for our tickets.
_____

5 I'm really looking forward to see that film.
_____

5 ●●● Complete the text with the correct form of the verbs below.

be   choose   download   ~~film~~   get   make
practise   ride   see   visit

I love ¹*filming* videos of me and my friends. We all enjoy
² _____ our BMX bikes, and some of the tricks we
can do look great when you film them. I always try
³ _____ interesting places for the videos – next
month we're planning ⁴ _____ a big park in London
to make a film there. I've asked all my friends
⁵ _____ their tricks so they can do them really well.
I'm really looking forward to ⁶ _____ the results.
My friends all tell me I'm quite good at ⁷ _____
videos. I wouldn't mind ⁸ _____ a job with
a film company when I'm older. I'd love ⁹ _____
a famous film director one day!
Click here if you want ¹⁰ _____ some of my videos
and watch them. I hope you enjoy them!

6 Complete the sentences with the words below. Then match sentences 1–3 with meanings a–c.

OUT of class

really   taking   upside

1 ☐ It's _____ ages.
2 ☐ It's _____ down.
3 ☐ It's _____ annoying.

a The top is at the bottom.
b It's making me feel angry.
c I'm spending a lot of time on it.

I can identify specific detail in a radio programme and talk about using technology.

1 **Choose the correct option.**

1 I get up for school at 7 *a.m.* / *p.m.*
2 There are sixty seconds in *a minute* / *an hour*.
3 I often see my friends *in* / *at* the weekend.
4 I usually text my grandma *once* / *once time* a week.
5 My brother usually gets up late *at* / *on* Sundays.
6 I sometimes watch TV *in* / *on* the evening.

2 **Match 1–6 with a–f to make sentences.**

1 ☐ We have our lunch in the canteen
2 ☐ The show is on TV three
3 ☐ My brother sometimes goes to bed at
4 ☐ I sometimes feel tired in
5 ☐ I only see my grandparents twice
6 ☐ I sometimes go shopping on

a a Saturday.   d midnight.
b the afternoon.   e a year.
c times a week.   f at lunch time.

3 **How often do you do these things? Write sentences.**

1 text friends
  I text friends every day.
2 chat with friends
  _____
3 find information online
  _____
4 download songs
  _____
5 listen to the radio
  _____
6 watch TV shows online
  _____
7 upload photos
  _____
8 print photos
  _____

4 🔊 **02 Listen to the first part of a radio programme. What is the programme about?**

a some people who are trying some new technology for a month
b some people who are not using technology for a month

5 🔊 **03 Listen to the second part of the programme. Mark the sentences T (true) or F (false).**

1 ☐ Isla is often bored in the evenings because she can't chat with her friends.
2 ☐ Isla is spending more time on her homework now.
3 ☐ Ben can't listen to music at the moment.
4 ☐ Ben doesn't like any of his parents' music.
5 ☐ Sara is watching more TV because she can't go online.
6 ☐ Isla is enjoying having printed photos.

6 🔊 **04 Complete what Isla says with the words below. Listen and check.**

| boring   online   terrible   usually   with

I'm finding it really difficult. I ¹_____ text my friends and chat ²_____ them a lot, but of course, now I can't do that. It's OK during the day, but the evenings are a bit ³_____. And the worst thing is trying to do homework. I can't go ⁴_____ to find information and that's ⁵_____! Books are OK, but it's much slower without the internet.

How can we have fun if no one can see what we're doing?

I can make and respond to suggestions.

1 Complete the responses in the dialogues with the words below.

| cool ~~great~~ rather sure why

1 A: Why don't you add some music to the video?

B: Yes, *great* idea.

2 A: You could buy a better camera.

B: I'd _____ not. They're very expensive!

3 A: Why don't you use your brother's video camera?

B: I'm not _____. He doesn't like people using his things.

4 A: Let's make a video about football.

B: Yes, _____ not?

5 A: Shall we go to the park?

B: OK, _____.

2 Write the responses from Exercise 1 in the correct column.

Accepting a suggestion	Rejecting a suggestion
Yes, great idea.	_____
_____	_____

3 Match suggestions 1–5 with responses a–e.

1 [c] Let's make a film about skateboarding.

2 [ ] You could use the camera on your phone.

3 [ ] Let's go into town now.

4 [ ] Why don't you ask someone to help you?

5 [ ] Shall we meet at six o'clock?

a I'm not sure. It doesn't take very good photos.

b I'd rather not. I want to do it myself.

c ~~Great idea! We're both really good at it!~~

d OK, cool. See you then.

e Why not? We might meet some friends there.

4 🔊 05 Complete the dialogue with sentences a–e. Listen and check.

Joe: Right, we want to film a video. What's the best idea?

Ann: [1]c

Joe: Hmm, I'm not sure. I can't do many tricks on my skateboard. I think it might be boring.

Ann: OK. Well, shall we make a video about dancing? I can ask some of my friends. Tara's a really good dancer.

Joe: [2]___

Ann: Well, we could make a funny video about your cat.

Joe: [3]___

Ann: Hmm, but he might not do anything funny in front of the camera.

Joe: [4]___

Ann: With you playing the guitar?

Joe: Yes.

Ann: [5]___

Joe: Cool! And we can ask Tom to sing.

Ann: Great! Let's do that!

a Yes, why not? He's always doing funny things.

b I'd rather not. I'd prefer to make a funny video.

c ~~Well, what about making a video about skateboarding?~~

d That's a great idea. I can play the drums, too.

e That's true. Why don't we make a music video?

5 Match sentences 1–3 with responses a–c.

OUT of class

1 [ ] Look, this is my new tablet.

2 [ ] Let's have pizza for lunch.

3 [ ] That's it! I'm leaving!

a Come back!

b This is so cool!

c Good idea. That's my favourite!

I can describe places and lifestyles.

1 Complete Matt's article for his school magazine with the words below.

evening   got   ~~home~~   usually   view   weekdays

My unusual lifestyle

by Matt Thompson

Most people live in a house or flat, **but** my [1] *home* is in a boat. I always have a [2] _____ of water! It's [3] _____ three bedrooms **and** a small living area. There's a kitchen and a bathroom too. **Although** it's small, it's warm and comfortable. We haven't got much technology. **However**, I've got a tablet **in case** I want to go online to chat with friends or watch films in the [4] _____ .

I live with my parents and my sister. We [5] _____ stay in one place during school time. I get up early on [6] _____ **because** I help look after the boat. We don't have a car, so I always walk to school. In the school holidays, we travel around. I like this lifestyle because I visit interesting places. **Also**, I meet lots of different people – **as well as** my school friends, I've got friends all over the country!

2 Read the text again. Mark the sentences T (true) or F (false).

1 ☐ Matt can't use the internet on his boat.
2 ☐ Four people live on Matt's boat.
3 ☐ Matt and his family never stay in one place for more than a few weeks.
4 ☐ Matt enjoys his lifestyle.

3 Match paragraphs 1–2 in the text with topics a–b.

a ☐ description of family and lifestyle
b ☐ description of home

4 Look at the words in bold in the text. Then choose the correct option.

1 My home isn't very big. *Although /* (*However,*) I enjoy living in it.
2 I meet lots of interesting people, *so / because* I never get bored.
3 There's an extra bed in the living area *as well as / in case* we want to invite friends to stay.
4 There's a living area inside the boat and there's space outside *as well as / too*.
5 *Although / However* my sister likes our lifestyle, she would prefer to live in a house.
6 Our lifestyle isn't expensive. *Too / Also*, it's good for the environment.

5 Complete Anna's notes about her home and lifestyle with the words below.

bedrooms   ~~camper van~~   get up   lifestyle
morning   never   tablet   university

HOME

- home: modern [1]camper van
- rooms: two [2]_____ , small kitchen and shower room
- small, quite comfortable, sometimes cold in the [3]_____
- TV; no internet connection, but have a [4]_____ I can use in cafés

FAMILY AND LIFESTYLE

- mum, dad and sister
- usually [5]_____ early – help with food and jobs
- [6]_____ go to school – study with mum and dad
- want to go to [7]_____ one day
- enjoy the way we live – travel all over the world
- interesting [8]_____ – meet lots of people

6 Write a description of Anna's home and lifestyle. Follow the instructions below.

1 Use the text in Exercise 1 as a model.
2 Write two paragraphs:
   - paragraph 1: Anna's home
   - paragraph 2: Anna's family and lifestyle.
3 Use connectors and time expressions.
4 Use the Present Simple.

1.8   SELF-ASSESSMENT

☺☺ = I understand and can help a friend.   ☹ = I understand but have some questions.

☺ = I understand and can do it by myself.   ☹☹ = I do not understand.

		☺☺	☺	☹	☹☹	Need help?	Now try ...
1.1	Vocabulary					Students' Book pp. 10–11 Workbook pp. 6–7	Ex. 1–2, p. 15
1.2	Grammar					Students' Book p. 12 Workbook p. 8	Ex. 3–4, p. 15
1.3	Reading					Students' Book p. 13 Workbook p. 9	
1.4	Grammar					Students' Book p. 14 Workbook p. 10	Ex. 5, p. 15
1.5	Listening					Students' Book p. 15 Workbook p. 11	
1.6	Speaking					Students' Book p. 16 Workbook p. 12	Ex. 6, p. 15
1.7	Writing					Students' Book p. 17 Workbook p. 13	

1.1 I can talk about everyday technology.

1.2 I can use different tenses to talk about the present.

1.3 I can find specific detail in an article and talk about unusual objects.

1.4 I can use verb constructions with *to*-infinitives and *-ing* forms.

1.5 I can identify specific detail in a radio programme and talk about using technology.

1.6 I can make and respond to suggestions.

1.7 I can describe places and lifestyles.

What can you remember from this unit?

New words I learned (the words you most want to remember from this unit)	**Expressions and phrases I liked** (any expressions or phrases you think sound nice, useful or funny)	**English I heard or read outside class** (e.g. from websites, books, adverts, films, music)

Vocabulary

1 Complete the words in the sentences.

1 My phone has no power – I need to find my **c** _ _ _ _ _ _ .

2 This **s** _ _ _ _ _ **s** _ _ _ _ is great for taking photos of yourself.

3 Do you usually **s** _ _ _ _ photos with your friends online?

4 I love music, so I **d** _ _ _ _ _ _ _ a lot of songs.

5 I hate that TV show – it's **a** _ _ _ _ _!

6 It's really hot and sunny today – it's a **p** _ _ _ _ _ _ _ day to go to the beach!

2 Complete the sentences with the words below. There is one extra word.

> break   evening   made   twice   ugly
> useful   weekend

1 I go swimming _____ a week, on Wednesdays and Fridays.

2 This is a very _____ gadget. I'd really like one.

3 I don't like this bag – it looks _____ .

4 Is that bag _____ of plastic?

5 At eleven o'clock our lessons stop because it's _____ time.

6 I often listen to music in the _____ .

Grammar

3 Complete the sentences with the Present Simple or Present Continuous form of the verbs in brackets.

1 Can you wait a minute? I _____ (chat) with my friends at the moment.

2 I _____ (not often/watch) films on my tablet – I prefer a bigger screen.

3 My uncle _____ (live) near the beach.

4 I _____ (not like) her music. I think it's boring!

5 It _____ (not rain) now, so we can go out.

6 Jake _____ (not want) to come to the party.

4 Complete the questions with the Present Simple or Present Continuous form of the verbs in brackets. Then complete the short answers.

1 A: _____ (you/often/read) e-books?
  B: No, I _____ . I prefer real books.

2 A: _____ (Jamie/listen) to music at the moment?
  B: Yes, he _____ . He's upstairs in his room.

3 A: _____ (you/think) it's a good film?
  B: Yes, I _____ . It's brilliant!

4 A: _____ (your friends/ make) a video today?
  B: Yes, they _____ . It's a music video.

5 A: _____ (you/do) your homework right now?
  B: No, I _____ . I'm too tired!

6 A: _____ (your friends/ always/remember) your birthday?
  B: No, they _____ . It's very annoying!

5 Choose the correct option.

1 Hurry up – I can't stand *to be / being* late!

2 George never offers *to pay / paying* for anything.

3 Please be quiet – I'm trying *to listen / listening* to music.

4 My parents allow me *to stay up / staying up* late at the weekend.

5 It's OK – I don't mind *to wait / waiting* for you.

6 Mike is hoping *to go / going* to art college.

Speaking language practice

6 Complete the dialogue with one word in each gap.

A: [1] _____ we organise something for Alana's birthday?

B: Yes, great [2] _____ . We [3] _____ have a party.

A: I'm not [4] _____ . A party's quite expensive. [5] _____ don't we go for a pizza?

B: I'd rather [6] _____ . I don't really like pizza.

A: OK, well, [7] _____ about a film night at my house?

B: Yes, why [8] _____ ? [9] _____ 's do that.

1 Match the words below with the pictures.

> ~~chat with friends~~   play games   send messages
> share photos   watch videos

1   *chat with friends*

2   _____

3   _____

4   _____

5   _____

2 Match 1–4 with a–d to make word friends.

1   [*d*] video   a   messages
2   [ ] social   b   device
3   [ ] instant   c   media
4   [ ] digital   d   ~~clip~~

3 Complete the sentences with the word friends in Exercise 2. Then tick (✓) the sentences that are true for you. Change the other sentences to make them true for you.

1   I use a lot of *social media*: Twitter, Facebook, Instagram …
2   I have a great new _____ : my tablet!
3   I like sending _____ when I'm working on my computer. It's very convenient.
4   I spend a lot time watching _____ on YouTube. I'm almost an addict!

4 Choose the correct option.

1   Korean children are good at *seeing* / (*solving*) problems together.
2   We *receive* / *require* information in different ways these days.
3   You can *access* / *acquire* the internet with many different devices.
4   The internet is *challenging* / *transforming* society.
5   If you *take* / *touch* the screen, some new information appears.
6   If you *switch* / *click* on the link, a new page opens.

5 Make sentences using verb + *to-*infinitive or verb + *-ing*.

1   I / not / plan / solve / the problem today
    I'm not planning to solve the problem today.
2   I / prefer / access / the internet at home
    _____
3   the internet / good at / transform / society
    _____
4   you / can practise / touch / the screen now
    _____
5   I would like / receive / more information online
    _____
6   try / click / on that link
    _____

6 Complete the definitions with the adjectives below.

> anxious   ~~funny~~   proficient
> smart   superficial

1   Someone or something that you makes you laugh is *funny*.
2   Someone or something that is intelligent is _____ .
3   Something that is not meaningful or complete is _____ .
4   Someone who is very worried is
    _____ .
5   Someone who is very good at something is _____ .

7 Which of the adjectives in Exercise 6 have a positive meaning? Which have a negative meaning? Write P or N.

8 Read the video script. Underline any words or phrases you don't know and find their meaning in your dictionary.

Addicted to screens

Part 1

How long do you spend online every day? Is this increasing at the moment? And when you're online, what do you do there – chat with friends, listen to music, watch videos, play games,
5 send messages? Can you do them all at the same time?
The internet is transforming our society too. It has a huge impact on culture, politics and business.
Now there are 'screenagers' who live most of their lives in the virtual world. Some people spend more time online than with
10 their families!
And this is the country where people are connected more than anywhere else in the world: South Korea. Here you can access the internet very easily, and it's really fast. You can download files ten times quicker here than in most countries in the world.
15 Even young children of three to five years old use the internet and spend eight hours a week online.
Then there are teenagers using the internet for eighteen hours a day. Experts say that if you take away the internet from these teens, they start to feel anxious and unhappy.
20 So, is Korea creating a nation of screen addicts? And will your country be like this in just two or three years' time?

Part 2

But is internet addiction a bad thing? Think for a moment about the information that you receive on screens. It's certainly not like
25 reading a book. Now we receive information via connections or hyperlinks. We just click on the link or touch the screen and something new appears.
And what about the videos of pets you watch on YouTube? You think it's funny or superficial, but this is part of a big online
30 conversation. You can watch the angry cat and then create your own clip or meme with a different cat. Sharing these photos and videos is more important than the content itself. It allows us to communicate with people in a more creative way.
So, do smartphones make us smarter or less smart? Let's return
35 to Korea for an answer. There's good news: Korea is the most connected country in the world, but it is also number one for education. It is regularly top of the world's education league tables. The reason may be that from an early age, Korean children are proficient at working together on the internet to
40 solve problems.

2

Wild nature

I can talk about the weather and natural disasters.

1 ● Complete the weather words.

Noun	Adjective
snow	[1]sn o w y
[2]s _ _ _	sunny
fog	[3]f _ _ _ _ _
[4]c _ _ _ _ _	cloudy
wind	[5]w _ _ _ _
[6]i _ _ _	icy
storm	[7]s _ _ _ _ _

2 ●● Choose the correct answers.

1 We don't want to drive because it's _____ today, so you can't see very well.
  a ice   b icy   c fog   ⓓ foggy

2 We can't go out in our boat because it's _____ and the sea is rough.
  a sun   b sunny   c storm   d stormy

3 It's very cold here in winter and there's often _____ on the ground.
  a snow   b snowy   c rain   d rainy

4 Look, it's a lovely _____ day. Let's go swimming in the sea!
  a sun   b sunny   c wind   d windy

5 You should drive slowly when there's _____ on the roads.
  a storm   b stormy   c ice   d icy

6 There's a lovely blue sky today – it isn't _____ at all.
  a sun   b sunny   c cloud   d cloudy

7 Sometimes things blow away when it's very _____.
  a wind   b windy   c ice   d icy

8 Everything in the garden gets wet when it's _____.
  a cloud   b cloudy   c rain   d rainy

3 ●● Find and correct the mistakes in the sentences. One sentence is correct.

1 It very foggy today.
  It's very foggy today.

2 Oh no! It getting cloudy!

_____

3 The sun is shine today.

_____

4 Look, it's snowy. Let's build a snowman!

_____

5 It's getting a bit storm now.

_____

4 ● Choose the correct answers.

1 Which word do we use for '-' in -10?
   (a) minus   b less   c lower

2 Which word does NOT mean 'hot'?
   a warm   b boiling   c chilly

3 Which word does NOT mean 'cold'?
   a mild   b cool   c freezing

4 Which word do we use to say '°' in 35°?
   a hot   b degrees   c temperature

5 ●● Choose the correct option.

1 Put your coat on – it's *freezing* / *mild* outside!

2 It's a nice *chilly* / *warm* day, so we can sit outside.

3 It's often *hot boiling* / *boiling hot* here in the summer.

4 The water's a bit *cool* / *mild*, but it's not too cold.

5 It's *lower* / *minus* fifteen here, so it's very cold!

6 Sometimes the temperature reaches forty *points* / *degrees* in the summer.

6 ● Complete the natural disaster words.

1 ea*r*thqu*a* *ke*
2 dr__ _g_t
3 fl__ _d
4 ts__ _ __mi
5 a_a_ _ __che
6 h__rr_ _ __ne

7 ● Complete the crossword.

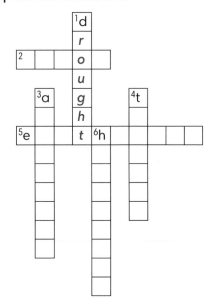

Across

2 when a lot of water covers the land

5 when the ground shakes

Down

1 when there is no rain for a long time and the ground becomes very dry

3 when a lot of snow falls from a mountain

4 when a very big wave comes from the sea onto the land

6 when there is a very strong wind

8 ●●● Read what four people say about the weather in their area. Choose the correct option.

It's a horrible wet, [1]*rainy* / *sunny* day here in Manchester, so you need your umbrella. It's also quite [2]*chilly* / *boiling*, so you definitely need your coat.

Sometimes we have [3]*earthquakes* / *floods* here and our house shakes. It's quite scary. I live near the sea, so when this happens, we always worry that there might be [4]*an avalanche* / *a tsunami* too.

Winters are usually [5]*boiling* / *freezing* cold where I live and we often have lots of [6]*snow* / *snowy*. It's great because we can build snowmen, but the roads are dangerous because they're often [7]*cloudy* / *icy*.

Usually the summers are warm and [8]*sun* / *sunny* here, but this year it's quite [9]*cool* / *mild*. It's also quite rainy, so we're worried there might be a [10]*flood* / *hurricane*.

9 ●●● Complete the weather forecast with one word in each gap.

● ● ●

☁ Weather around the world

- In **Madrid** it's boiling [1]*hot* today and the sky is a lovely clear blue.

- In **London** it's quite cold and it's also starting to [2]_____ a bit windy, so hold onto your hats!

- In **Paris** the [3]_____ is shining and it's lovely and warm.

- It's a cold night in **Toronto**, with temperatures as low as [4]_____ 15.

- In northern **Australia** the [5]_____ continues. Plants are dying because it's so dry and everyone is hoping for some rain soon.

- In **New York** it's a lovely sunny day, with a temperature of around 25 [6]_____.

I can use regular and irregular verbs to talk about the past.

1 ● **Complete the sentences with the Past Simple form of the verbs in brackets.**

1 I was tired and I *wanted* (want) to go home.
2 I _____ (not enjoy) the film last night.
3 My dad _____ (study) Maths at university.
4 Ralph _____ (not help) us to organise the party last week.
5 I _____ (spot) Tim in the park yesterday.
6 Sara _____ (not look) very happy.

2 ● **Match infinitives 1–8 with their Past Simple forms a–h.**

1 [c] become   a met
2 [ ] see   b thought
3 [ ] feel   c became
4 [ ] think   d knew
5 [ ] take   e saw
6 [ ] meet   f went
7 [ ] go   g felt
8 [ ] know   h took

3 ●● **Complete the sentences with the Past Simple form of the pairs of verbs below.**

become, not go   feel, find   meet, not like
not take, visit   see, not know

1 We were scared when we *saw* the tsunami and we *didn't know* what to do.
2 Jake _____ many photos when he _____ Canada last year.
3 The storm soon _____ quite bad, so we _____ outside.
4 I _____ really happy when I finally _____ my bag again.
5 She _____ George last year, but she _____ him at first.

4 ●● **Complete the dialogues. Use the Past Simple.**

1 A: What film *did you see* last night?
   B: We saw *Spectre*.
2 A: When _____?
   B: The hurricane happened on Tuesday night.
3 A: Where _____ your coat?
   B: I put it in the kitchen.
4 A: _____ any photos of the storm?
   B: No, I didn't take any photos.
5 A: When _____ Mark?
   B: I met him last summer.

5 ●●● **Complete the post with the Past Simple form of the verbs below.**

become   come   feel   help   not sleep   not stop
not want   see   think   watch

Wow! What amazing weather! ¹*Did* you *see* the snowstorm last night? It started at about eight o'clock and at first I ²_____ it wasn't very bad. But the snow soon ³_____ quite thick on the ground. It ⁴_____ snowing for about five hours! I ⁵_____ at all because I ⁶_____ so excited – I ⁷_____ to miss anything! This morning some friends ⁸_____ round to our house and ⁹_____ us clear the snow away from our door. Thanks, guys! I don't know about the weather today. ¹⁰_____ you _____ the weather forecast on TV this morning? Let me know if you did!

added by Mike   Tweet 🐦 13   Like 2

6 ●●● **Complete the text with one word in each gap.**

Yes, I ¹*saw* the snowstorm ²_____ night – amazing! The last storm like this was five years ³_____ . It ⁴_____ place ⁵_____ December, right at the beginning of the winter. We made some amazing snowmen that year, but unfortunately, they ⁶_____ not last very long because the snow soon melted. I posted some photos yesterday, when the storm started. ⁷_____ you see them?

added by Leon   Tweet 🐦 13   Like 2

I can find specific detail in a text and talk about culture.

1 **WORD FRIENDS** Choose the word that does NOT fit in each sentence.

1 You look _____ ridiculous in that hat!
   (a) very   b completely   c absolutely

2 My brother is _____ crazy!
   a absolutely   b completely   c very

3 Sam is _____ good at English.
   a very   b really   c totally

4 That lesson was _____ interesting.
   a completely   b quite   c really

5 This place is _____ amazing!
   a quite   b absolutely   c totally

6 It's usually _____ cold here in winter.
   a really   b quite   c totally

2 Read the forum posts. Match headings 1–4 with posts A–D.

1 ☐ Extreme heat
2 ☐ On top of the world
3 ☐ River adventure
4 ☐ A wild place close to home

3 Read the texts again. Match people 1–5 with phrases a–f to make true sentences. There is one extra phrase.

1 ☐ Max   4 ☐ Paul's uncle
2 ☐ Emma   5 ☐ Paul
3 ☐ Sara

a lives in a place where there are sometimes natural disasters.
b was happy with the weather during a trip.
c enjoyed a very active holiday.
d had a problem while on a trip.
e wants to travel to a place that a relative visited.
f enjoyed learning about the history of a place.

4 Complete the phrases from the text. Then match them with definitions a–e.

1 ☐ *d*   *very* wild   a fairly hot
2 ☐ _____ stunning   b not very cold
3 ☐ _____ warm   c very interesting
4 ☐ _____ mild   d ~~with few people living there~~
5 ☐ _____ fascinating   e very beautiful

● ● ●

WILD PLACES
There are hundreds of amazing places to visit in the world. Tell us about your experiences!

A Last summer I went to Tibet with my family. We were in a very wild area high up in the Himalayas. It was a walking holiday, so we walked and climbed every day – sometimes up to over 4,000 metres! It's really beautiful in the summer, but in winter it's very dangerous because there's a lot of snow and there's always a possibility of avalanches. The local people believe that human-like creatures called yeti live in the mountains, but we didn't see any!   *Max*

B I live in the town of Moteuka in New Zealand, near the Abel Tasman National Park. The park is named after Abel Tasman, one of the first Europeans to reach New Zealand. It's an amazing wild place. There are forests where you can walk and camp, and some absolutely stunning beaches. I swam in the sea last week and it was really warm. Winter is quite mild and summer isn't too hot. There are a lot of earthquakes in New Zealand, but they aren't usually very bad in this area.   *Emma*

C In July I travelled to Death Valley in the USA. It's a very dry place, with almost no rain for most of the year, so there aren't many plants. It's absolutely boiling in summer, with temperatures over fifty degrees! We learned about what life was like here in the past – that was absolutely fascinating. The first Europeans who arrived called it Death Valley because without water, you can't live there for very long!   *Sara*

D My uncle went on an adventure holiday to South America last year. He travelled by boat through the rainforest of Brazil. He went in July, so it was really hot, but there wasn't too much rain because it was the dry season – he was pleased about that! He saw some really colourful birds and monkeys too. He didn't see any dangerous animals though. The photos he took are absolutely amazing! Some people still live a traditional life in the forest. Scientists are trying to learn from them how to use all the plants in the forest as medicines. I'd love to go there one day!   *Paul*

I can talk about an event in the past and what was happening around it.

1 ● Complete the sentences with the Past Continuous form of the verbs in brackets.

1 He found some unusual plants while he _was visiting_ (visit) Mexico.
2 They _____ (not listen) when the guide explained the dangers of eating wild plants.
3 What _____ (you/do) when you saw the avalanche?
4 They _____ (swim) in the sea when they saw the shark.
5 _____ (it/rain) when you left home?
6 Someone took my camera while I _____ (not look).

2 ● Choose the correct option.

1 I was running for the bus when I (dropped)/ was dropping my phone.
2 Jack fell asleep while he _watched / was watching_ the film.
3 We were walking home when the wind _started / was starting_ to get stronger.
4 My cousins _stayed / were staying_ in Japan when the earthquake happened.
5 The bear _appeared / was appearing_ while we were walking down the mountain.
6 The postman _came / was coming_ while we were having breakfast.

3 ●● Complete the sentences with the Past Simple or Past Continuous form of the verbs in brackets.

1 We _saw_ (see) something strange in the sky while we _were looking_ (look) at the stars.
2 The sun _____ (shine) when we _____ (arrive) at the beach.
3 While I _____ (wait) for the bus, I _____ (text) a few friends.
4 Jenna _____ (cry) when I finally _____ (find) her.
5 We first _____ (hear) about the storm while we _____ (have) dinner.
6 When I _____ (arrive) at Paula's house, she _____ (sit) outside in her garden.

4 ●● Complete the sentences with _when_ or _while_.

1 I hurt my arm _while_ I was playing tennis yesterday.
2 Jess was waiting for us _____ we got home.
3 We stayed inside _____ the snow was falling.
4 _____ my phone rang, I was watching TV.
5 The weather changed suddenly _____ we were thinking about what to do.

5 ●●● Complete the dialogue with the Past Simple or Past Continuous form of the verbs below.

> climb do eat fall find (x2) have (x2) look for lose not stop shine start

A: ¹_Did_ you _have_ a good time on your Geography trip last week?
B: Yes, we ²_____ a great time in the morning while the sun ³_____. But it ⁴_____ to rain while we ⁵_____ our lunch, and it ⁶_____ for the rest of the day!
A: Oh dear! Where ⁷_____ you _____ these amazing rocks?
B: I ⁸_____ them while we ⁹_____ plants near the river.
A: They're lovely. But it's a pity about your camera. What ¹⁰_____ you _____ when you ¹¹_____ it?
B: I ¹²_____ over some rocks when I ¹³_____ and dropped it into the river.

6 Order the words in a–b to make phrases. Then use the phrases to complete sentences 1–2.

OUT of class

a accident / was / an / it
_____

b funny / time / was / at / it / the
_____

1 We all laughed when he fell in the water. I know it was dangerous, but _____.

2 I'm sorry, I didn't mean to break the plate – _____.

I can identify specific detail in a conversation about an activity camp.

1 Look at the pictures and complete the words.

1 w_a_t_e_r_f_a_l_l_   2 s_ _ _ _ _ _ _

3 s_ _ _ _ _ _   4 l_ _ _ _ _ _

5 b_ _ _ _   6 b_ _ _

2 Complete the sentences with the words below. There is one extra word.

| path ~~cave~~ bat stars wildlife sky

1 It was very dark at the back of the _cave_.
2 At night you can see the _____ shining.
3 There is a lot of interesting _____ in the forest.
4 We followed the _____ until we came to a river.
5 There were only a few clouds in the _____.

3 **WORD FRIENDS** Match 1–6 with a–f to make sentences.

1 [d] It was raining, so we made
2 ☐ It was cold, so we made
3 ☐ I really want to learn
4 ☐ It's too cold to sleep
5 ☐ Last year scientists discovered
6 ☐ We looked

a about the wildlife in the forest.
b some interesting plants here.
c a fire to keep warm.
d ~~a shelter to keep us dry.~~
e for wild animals, but didn't find any.
f outside.

4 🔊 06 Listen to the first part of a conversation. What kind of summer camp did Alex go on?

a extreme fitness
b survival skills
c discovering wildlife

5 🔊 07 Listen to the second part of the conversation. Match people 1–4 with activities a–f. There are two extra activities.

1 ☐ Alex   3 ☐ Dan
2 ☐ Chloe   4 ☐ Alex's mum

a was cold at night
b tried to make a fire
c worried about finding water
d needs a comfortable place to sleep
e got lost at night
f caught a fish

I can criticise and explain when things go wrong.

1 Complete the sentences with the words below.

> mean   wanted   careful   realise   ~~thinking~~

1 What were you *thinking* of?
2 I didn't _____ to.
3 Just be more _____ next time.
4 I really _____ to make you laugh.
5 I'm sorry, I didn't _____ .

2 Order the words to make sentences.

1 for / do / what / you / that / did / ?
   What did you do that for?
2 thought / I / asleep / you / were
   _____
3 do / why / you / that / did / ?
   _____
4 hurt / didn't / you / mean / I / to
   _____
5 wanted / really / to / help / I
   _____

3 Write the phrases below in the correct column.

> I didn't mean to …   I didn't realise.
> ~~I really wanted to …~~   I thought you were …
> Just be more careful next time.
> What did you do that for?
> What were you thinking of?
> Why did you do that?

Criticising

Explaining
I really wanted to …

4 Choose the correct responses.

1 You lost my phone! Why did you do that?
   a I thought it was your phone.
   (b) I didn't mean to lose it.
   c Just be more careful next time.

2 Surprise! Look at this big spider!
   a I didn't mean to scare you.
   b Oh, I'm sorry. I didn't realise.
   c Why did you do that? You know I hate spiders!

3 I'm sorry my football broke your window.
   a Well, just be more careful next time.
   b What did you do that for?
   c Oh, I didn't realise.

4 You used my bike without asking me! What were you thinking of?
   a Why did you do that?
   b I'm sorry. I thought it was OK to use it.
   c Just be more careful next time.

5 🔊 08 Complete the dialogues with one word in each gap. Listen and check.

1
Ella: Jack, where's my concert ticket from last night?
Jack: I put it in the bin.
Ella: [1]*Why* did you do that?
Jack: I [2]_____ you didn't want it.
Ella: Of course I want it – I want to keep it as a souvenir!

2
Tom: What's all this mess?
Lisa: Err, I was trying to do some cooking and things went a bit wrong …
Tom: What were you [3]_____ of? Mum's coming home soon.
Lisa: I didn't [4]_____ to make a mess.
Tom: Come on, I can help you clear it up.

3
Kim: Why is my jumper all wet?
Dora: I washed it for you.
Kim: What did you do that [5]_____ ?
Dora: Well, I wore it today and I dropped hot chocolate all over it.
Kim: Well, just be more [6]_____ next time – and don't wear my clothes without asking me!

I can use adverbs and indefinite pronouns.

1 Complete the table.

People	Things	Places
somebody	¹_something_	somewhere
² _____	nothing	³ _____
everybody	⁴ _____	everywhere
⁵ _____	anything	⁶ _____

2 Choose the correct option.

1 I want to go (somewhere) / something exciting next year.

2 He wants to invite everything / everybody to his party.

3 Is there something / anything to eat?

4 The streets were really busy – there were people everywhere / anywhere.

5 It's boring here – there's anything / nothing to do!

6 Cara doesn't have anybody / nobody to talk to.

7 Everybody like / likes chips!

8 There is / isn't nothing in the box.

3 Complete the sentences with indefinite pronouns.

1 I wasn't hungry so I didn't eat _anything_.

2 Don't tell _____ about this – it's a secret!

3 I looked _____ for my phone, but I didn't find it.

4 Can we stop for a minute? There's _____ in my shoe.

5 There's _____ for young people to go in this town – it's awful!

6 _____ stole my purse while I was waiting for the bus.

4 Complete the second sentence so that it means the same as the first sentence. Use no more than three words.

1 All the people at the concert were really happy.
Everybody at _the concert was_ really happy.

2 I haven't got anything to wear!
I _____ nothing to wear!

3 There was nowhere to sit down.
_____ anywhere to sit down.

4 All the things in the shop were expensive.
Everything in _____ expensive.

5 Read the text. Choose the correct answers.

A survival story

Last year Tyler Jackson and his friend Liam were walking in the mountains in Canada. It suddenly became very foggy, so they had to stop. Luckily, they knew ¹_____ about survival. First, they had to find water. You can't survive for long if you don't have ²_____ to drink. Luckily, they had food with them. If you have ³_____ to eat, you will soon get very cold up in the mountains. They then looked around for ⁴_____ safe to sleep and found a small cave. All their friends and family knew they were in the mountains, so they knew that ⁵_____ would call the mountain rescue service. Two days later the rescuers found them and ⁶_____ ended well.

1 a nothing   c̶ something
  b anything   d somewhere

2 a everything   c anywhere
  b nothing   d anything

3 a nothing   c nobody
  b anything   d everything

4 a somewhere   c anywhere
  b something   d anything

5 a anybody   c nobody
  b somebody   d something

6 a something   c everything
  b anything   d nothing

2.8 SELF-ASSESSMENT

For each learning objective, tick (✓) the box that best matches your ability.

☺☺ = I understand and can help a friend.　　　　☹ = I understand but have some questions.

☺ = I understand and can do it by myself.　　　　☹☹ = I do not understand.

		☺☺	☺	☹	☹☹	Need help?	Now try ...
2.1	Vocabulary					Students' Book pp. 22–23 Workbook pp. 18–19	Ex. 1–2, p. 27
2.2	Grammar					Students' Book p. 24 Workbook p. 20	Ex. 3, p. 27
2.3	Reading					Students' Book p. 25 Workbook p. 21	
2.4	Grammar					Students' Book p. 26 Workbook p. 22	Ex. 4–5, p. 27
2.5	Listening					Students' Book p. 27 Workbook p. 23	
2.6	Speaking					Students' Book p. 28 Workbook p. 24	Ex. 7, p. 27
2.7	English in Use					Students' Book p. 29 Workbook p. 25	Ex. 6, p. 27

2.1　I can talk about the weather and natural disasters.
2.2　I can use regular and irregular verbs to talk about the past.
2.3　I can find specific detail in a text and talk about culture.
2.4　I can talk about an event in the past and what was happening around it.
2.5　I can identify specific detail in a conversation about an activity camp.
2.6　I can criticise and explain when things go wrong.
2.7　I can use adverbs and indefinite pronouns.

What can you remember from this unit?

New words I learned (the words you most want to remember from this unit)	**Expressions and phrases I liked** (any expressions or phrases you think sound nice, useful or funny)	**English I heard or read outside class** (e.g. from websites, books, adverts, films, music)

Vocabulary

1 Complete the words in the sentences.

1 Look, it's a lovely **s**_____ day!
2 Some trees blew down in the strong **w**_____.
3 We couldn't see very well because it was **f**_____.
4 It's quite **m**_____ today, so you don't need a coat.
5 Shut the door! It's **f**_____ cold outside!
6 The temperature is twenty-seven **d**_____ today.
7 It rained for five days and there was a **f**_____ in our town.
8 Our school building shook during the **e**_____.

2 Choose the correct option.

1 The *stars / leaves* fall off the trees in winter.
2 We found a small *path / sky* going through the forest.
3 We tried to *have / make* a shelter, but it was too difficult.
4 Scientists *watched / discovered* some unusual plants near the river.
5 This book is *completely / really* interesting.
6 You won the game? That's *absolutely / very* fantastic!

Grammar

3 Complete the sentences with the Past Simple form of the verbs below.

| go   have   not see   not want   stay   take

1 I _____ at the activity camp for three weeks.
2 We spent three weeks in Iceland, but we _____ the Northern Lights.
3 I _____ swimming every day when I was on holiday.
4 His first concert _____ place in London last week.
5 She _____ to touch the spider.
6 _____ you _____ a good time on the Survival Weekend?

4 Complete the sentences with the Past Continuous form of the verbs in brackets.

1 I knew that my dad _____ (not watch) the film because his eyes were closed.
2 Lia hurt her knee while she _____ (swim) in the river.
3 They _____ (not chat) when I arrived.
4 A: _____ (the sun/shine) when you left home?
   B: Yes, it _____.
5 A: _____ (the bears/sleep) when you saw them?
   B: No, they _____. They were wide awake!

5 Choose the correct option.

1 I *saw / was seeing* a really big spider while I *walked / was walking* through the forest.
2 A lot of people *skied / were skiing* on the mountain when the avalanche *happened / was happening*.
3 We *watched / were watching* some amazing sunsets while we *stayed / were staying* in Scotland.
4 My brother *sat / was sitting* in the kitchen when I *got / was getting* home.
5 We *watched / were watching* TV *when / while* the hurricane started.

6 Choose the correct answers.

1 I'm cold – I want to go _____ warm!
   a something   b everywhere   c somewhere
2 I'm really bored – there's _____ to do here!
   a anything   b nothing   c something
3 He's a very popular singer. _____ loves his music!
   a Everybody   b Anybody   c Somebody
4 I'm lonely because I haven't got _____ to talk to.
   a nobody   b anybody   c somebody

Speaking language practice

7 Complete the dialogues with the phrases below.

| be more careful   I didn't mean to   I didn't realise
| I really wanted   why did you do that

A
A: Where's my bike?
B: I said that Jo could use it today.
A: ¹_____? I need it today.
B: Sorry, ²_____ you needed it.
B
A: Oh look – the pizzas are burnt!
B: Sorry, ³_____ burn them.
   ⁴_____ to help, so I put them in the oven.
A: Well, just ⁵_____ next time.

1 Match the words below with the photos.

> freak snowstorm   grey skies   high winds
> sunny climate   torrential rain   tropical storm

1   *freak snowstorm*   2 _____

3 _____   4 _____

5 _____   6 _____

2 What countries have the weather conditions in Exercise 1?

snowstorms: Iceland

3 Complete the sentences with the words below.

> chaotic   chasers   devastation   extremes
> factors   forecaster

1   It's difficult to be a weather *forecaster* in the UK because the weather is always changing!
2   In the USA they have great _____ of weather.
3   Storm _____ follow storms and warn people of the danger.
4   Tornadoes can cause damage and _____.
5   Snowstorms can bring _____ conditions to the roads and railways.
6   Economic and social _____ may influence our character more than the weather.

4 Complete the sentences with the Past Simple or Past Continuous of the verbs in brackets.

1   These men *were fishing* (fish) without any problem in the ocean, but suddenly, they _____ (decide) to turn back.
2   This young dolphin _____ (swim) with its group when it _____ (get) separated in a big wave.
3   The storm _____ (hit) when the people in the village _____ (go) to bed.
4   Torrential rain _____ (arrive) while the people _____ (build) a big shelter.
5   We _____ (travel) by boat when a huge whale _____ (hit) the side and the boat _____ (start) to sink.

5 Write the opposite of the underlined adjectives. Use the words below.

> deep   rough   torrential   ugly   warm

1   The water is <u>shallow</u>, so it's very easy to swim. *deep*
2   The seascape is <u>beautiful</u>, with lots of colourful corals. _____
3   The rain is <u>light</u> – you can definitely go out in it. _____
4   The sea is really <u>calm</u> right now – you can easily go swimming. _____
5   The air is <u>cool</u> today – perfect for a nice walk! _____

6 Choose the correct option.

1   The sunset was (absolutely) / very fantastic yesterday.
2   This exercise is *totally / really* difficult.
3   The video about the Atlantic was *completely / quite* good.
4   There are lot of videos on YouTube which are *completely / very* crazy.
5   The weather where I live is usually *really / totally* nice.

7 Read the video script. Underline any words or phrases you don't know and find their meaning in your dictionary.

Severe weather

Part 1

This is the wildest ocean on Earth! It is home to totally amazing marine life: penguins, seals, whales, dolphins and sharks – and people who battle the roughest seas. It stretches 16,000 km from
5 its shallow waters in the sunny tropics to the deep dark waters of the Arctic and Antarctic. It is an ocean of great extremes. It is unpredictable and dangerous, but at the same time absolutely beautiful. This is a strange paradise! Welcome to the Atlantic!

Part 2

10 This is Cape Verde, a group of islands off the coast of Africa. Here hot winds from the Sahara Desert have made the sea turn wild. The waves are huge and the conditions are difficult. These men were fishing without any problem in the ocean. But suddenly, they decided to turn back. It was too dangerous to
15 continue.
Winds like this cross the Atlantic quickly. Warm air rises from the sea and creates black clouds. A vortex then forms and the water of the ocean spins around very fast. The storm crosses the ocean very quickly and it grows stronger with every mile. At 120 km per
20 hour, this storm is now a hurricane! It's an unstoppable force of nature and is now moving towards the Caribbean. Dolphins swim to deeper water. They must stay together through the storm. Torrential rain arrives on land and enormous waves and strong winds cause devastation. Paradise is now hell!

25 ### Part 3

This hurricane was particularly strong. Here in the Bahamas it destroyed houses, trees and businesses, but the people were able to escape.
However, in the sea there is no protection for the animals.
30 Hurricanes break up dolphin groups. Somewhere in the ocean this young dolphin was swimming with its group when it was separated from the others in a big wave. Now it's at risk from a shark attack. Here a manatee finds safety in a mangrove forest. In fact, these underwater forests protect this area very well from storms
35 because the vegetation is so thick.
Soon the coral reefs recover and our young dolphin is reunited with the group.
And so life in the Tropical Atlantic returns to normal. The stormy conditions will come again, but for now all is calm in paradise.

3

The taste test

VOCABULARY
Food and drinks | Flavours |
Describing food

GRAMMAR
Present Perfect with *ever, never,
just, already, yet, for* and *since* |
Present Perfect and Past Simple

READING
Multiple choice

LISTENING
Identifying specific detail |
True/False

SPEAKING
Ordering food

WRITING
An email to a friend

BBC CULTURE
What do the British really eat?

I can talk about food and drink.

1 ● Find eight food and drink words in the word search and write them below.

H	O	N	E	Y	N	G	A	P	L
W	M	Z	A	X	G	S	N	E	E
A	C	R	I	S	P	S	U	D	M
S	R	B	I	A	E	O	T	F	O
O	E	O	S	B	A	K	S	E	N
M	A	R	N	R	C	L	C	C	A
E	M	I	C	O	H	L	H	T	D
F	A	Y	O	G	H	U	R	T	E
L	E	T	T	U	C	E	O	E	H
A	A	E	V	N	O	I	C	L	N

1 h o n e y   5 c _ _ _ _ m
2 c _ _ _ _ _ s   6 p _ _ _ _ h
3 y _ _ _ _ _ _ t   7 n _ _ s
4 l _ _ _ _ _ e   8 l _ _ _ _ _ _ e

2 ● Choose the correct answers.

1 Which one is NOT a fruit?
   (a) garlic   b pear   c pineapple

2 Which one is a kind of meat?
   a flour   b beef   c cheese

3 Which one is NOT a drink?
   a ice cream   b smoothie   c lemonade

4 Which one is a dairy food?
   a honey   b tuna   c cheese

5 Which one is NOT a vegetable?
   a lettuce   b cucumber   c grapes

6 Which one is NOT sweet?
   a honey   b crisps   c chewing gum

7 Which one makes you feel hot?
   a chilli   b bread rolls c ice cream

3 ●● Match descriptions 1–7 with foods a–g.

1 [c] It's a vegetable you use in salads.   a flour
2 [ ] It's a drink made with fruit.   b tuna
3 [ ] It's a large fruit.   c ~~cucumber~~
4 [ ] It's a kind of fish.   d ice cream
5 [ ] You eat them as a snack.   e smoothie
6 [ ] You use it to make bread.   f crisps
7 [ ] It's a cold, sweet food.   g pineapple

4 ●● Choose the correct option.

1 I always drink *cheese /* ~~*fruit juice*~~ in the morning.
2 I love fruit, especially *garlic / grapes*.
3 My sister doesn't agree with killing animals for food, so she doesn't eat *beef / peach*.
4 *Lettuce / Lemonade* is my favourite drink!
5 I sometimes add *cheese / honey* to yoghurt to make it taste sweet.
6 You can add *chilli / cream* to food to give it a hot taste.

5 ●● Complete the sentences with the words below.

| bread roll   cheese   chewing gum   garlic
| ~~nuts~~   pear

1 *Nuts* are a healthy snack.
2 My sister likes a lot of _____ on her pizza, but I don't like dairy foods.
3 I had a lovely warm _____ for breakfast.
4 We aren't allowed to have _____ in our mouth when we're in class.
5 Would you prefer an apple or a _____?
6 You can add _____ to food to give a strong flavour.

6 ●● Order the letters and complete the words in the sentences.

What's your favourite ice cream flavour?

1 I like fruit flavours like *melon* (emoln) and _____ (wabesrtrry).

2 My favourite ice cream flavours are _____ (lacohotec) and _____ (laivlna). Mmm!

3 I love _____ (mtni) because it's a lovely cool flavour.

4 I like _____ (menlo) flavour because it isn't sweet.

5 _____ (nccootu) is definitely my favourite! I like _____ (foecef) as a drink, but I hate it as an ice cream flavour.

7 ●●● Complete what the people say about food and drink with the words below.

| ~~bread roll~~   crisps   fruit juice   lettuce
| strawberry   yoghurt

●●●

I usually eat a [1]*bread roll* with butter and jam for breakfast, and drink a glass of [2]_____ – apple is my favourite. For lunch, I often have a salad with [3]_____ and cucumber or maybe a sandwich. I don't eat many snacks like [4]_____ because they aren't good for you. If I'm hungry, I often have a fruit [5]_____ – my favourite flavour is [6]_____!

| beef   nuts   pineapple   smoothie
| tuna   vanilla

●●●

I'm a vegetarian, so I don't eat meat such as [7]_____. I eat fish, though, especially [8]_____! I try to eat a lot of fruit because it's good for you – my favourite fruit is [9]_____. Sometimes I use lots of different kinds of fruit to make a [10]_____ – it's my favourite drink. I usually try to eat healthy snacks like [11]_____, but I also love [12]_____ ice cream!

8 ●●● Choose the correct option.

A

A: Mmm, I love this [1]~~chocolate~~/ *flour cake*! Did you make it?
B: Yes, I did. I used [2]*garlic / honey* to make it nice and sweet. Shall I pour some [3]*crisps / cream* on it for you?
A: Oh yes, please!

B

A: Do you like the [4]*lemonade / lemon* ice cream?
B: Yes, it's OK, but I think the [5]*coconut / coconuts* ice cream is nicer.

C

A: This meat is nice. It tastes quite hot.
B: That's because I added some [6]*chilli / cheese*. Maybe next time I should add some herbs like [7]*melon / mint* to make it taste cooler!

I can use the Present Perfect with *ever, never, just, already* and *yet*.

1 ● **Complete the sentences with the Present Perfect form of the verbs in brackets.**

1 I *'ve invited* (invite) all my friends to the party.
2 Sam _____ (not decide) what to do yet.
3 _____ (you/try) mint ice cream?
4 We _____ (not have) lunch yet.
5 Sasha _____ (eat) noodles with chilli!
6 _____ (your dad/order) the pizzas yet?
7 I _____ (hear) his music before – it's really good.

2 ● **Rewrite the sentences putting the words in brackets in the correct place.**

1 Have you tried making bread? (ever)
   Have you ever tried making bread?

2 I've cooked noodles. (never)
   _____

3 Molly has left. (just)
   _____

4 We haven't finished eating. (yet)
   _____

5 I've had lunch. (already)
   _____

6 Have you watched his cookery show on TV? (ever)
   _____

7 Have you tried the pizza? (yet)
   _____

3 ●● **Make sentences in the Present Perfect. Use the words in brackets.**

1 you / meet / a famous chef / ? (ever)
   Have you ever met a famous chef?

2 the film / start (already)
   _____

3 your email / not arrive (yet)
   _____

4 you / make / Sara's birthday cake / ? (yet)
   _____

5 Mike / cook / a meal (never)
   _____

6 we / order / our food (just)
   _____

4 ●● **Choose the correct option.**

1 Have you (ever) / yet eaten chilli ice cream?
2 I've *never / already* seen that film, so I don't want to see it again.
3 Have you cooked the pizza *yet / ever*?
4 Jo isn't here – she's *just / yet* left.
5 I've *ever / never* tried Chinese food.
6 I haven't finished my homework *yet / already*.

5 ●●● **Complete the dialogues. Use the Present Perfect.**

A

A: ¹*Have you finished your homework yet?* (you/ finish/your homework/yet) ?

B: No, I ² _____ . But Tara ³ _____ (do/already) all the Maths exercises, so she can help me!

B

A: ⁴ _____ (you/try/ever) a vegetable smoothie?

B: Yes, I ⁵ _____ . I've got a smoothie maker, and I ⁶ _____ (make/just) a carrot and tomato smoothie – lovely!

C

A: ⁷ _____ (you/watch) that new cookery show on TV?

B: No, I ⁸ _____ (hear) people talking about it a lot, but I ⁹ _____ (never/see) it. Is it good?

A: Yes, it's great. I ¹⁰ _____ (learn/already) a lot just from watching the first two shows.

6 ●●● **Complete the email with one word in each gap.**

From: Niki;
To: Maria;

Hi Maria,

I hope you can still come round to my house later for the film night. I ¹'ve made some pizzas – yes, I made them myself! Have you ² _____ tried making your own pizza? It isn't difficult. I haven't tasted them ³ _____ because I've ⁴ _____ taken them out of the oven, so they're still really hot. I've also bought some coconut ice cream. I've ⁵ _____ tried this type before, so I hope it's nice. Jake ⁶ _____ emailed me to say he can come, which is great, but I ⁷ _____ heard from Cara ⁸ _____ . I hope she can come.

See you later!
Niki

I can find specific detail in an article and use *make* and *do* accurately.

1 Complete the sentences with the correct form of *make* or *do*.

1 Sam *makes* a lot of cakes.
2 _____ your homework now.
3 Have you _____ your decision yet?
4 Please don't _____ a mess in here!
5 You didn't win the competition, but you _____ your best, so well done!

2 Complete the sentences with nouns formed from the verbs below.

> appear build compete weigh

1 Their apartment is in a new *building*.
2 Laura spends a lot of money on clothes because her _____ is important to her.
3 No chocolate for me, thanks. I'm trying to lose _____.
4 We're having a cookery _____ at our school.

3 Read the article. Choose the correct answers.

1 Why did Dean first start making chocolates?
   a He wanted to earn some money.
   b He wanted a special present for a relative.
   c He was looking for a new hobby.
   d He wanted to win a competition.

2 What happened when he first tried to sell his chocolates?
   a Only his family and friends bought his chocolates.
   b He made too many chocolates and couldn't sell them all.
   c Family members had to help him make more chocolates quickly.
   d His prices were too high.

3 Why is his honey and chilli chocolate his favourite?
   a It makes the most money.
   b It is the most popular with his customers.
   c It's his most unusual flavour.
   d It was his own idea.

4 What are Dean's plans for the summer?
   a to work on some new chocolates to sell
   b to work for a chocolate-maker in his town
   c to visit France with his family
   d to go on holiday with friends

4 Write a sentence for each highlighted phrase in the article.

A passion for chocolate

Dean Pollard is seventeen and he runs a successful business, making delicious chocolates.

Dean has made chocolates since he was ten years old, but he didn't plan to make money from them at first. He just wanted to give his grandma something special for her birthday. He found that he enjoyed making chocolates and he soon started winning competitions. His parents were just pleased that his hobby didn't have a bad effect on his school work.

In the beginning, Dean just made chocolates for family and friends and he never asked for any money. But at the age of fifteen he decided to turn his passion into a business, so he set up a website. He kept his prices quite low, and the first weekend the website came online he was so busy that his parents had to help out so there were enough chocolates for all the customers! He soon decided to put his prices up!

Dean makes a huge range of chocolates with different flavours and he's especially proud of his more unusual flavours like his lemon coconut creams. Mint and strawberry are the most popular flavours with customers, but Dean is particularly proud of his honey and chilli chocolate, not because it makes a lot of money for him, but because it was the first flavour that he developed himself.

So, what are Dean's plans for the summer? A local chocolate-maker in his town has offered him the chance to work for them during the summer holiday, but Dean isn't interested in the job. He really wants to spend the summer working on some exciting new flavours for his chocolates. 'My friends have invited me to go to France with them, but I'm just too busy,' he says. 'Maybe next year!'

I can talk about duration of time and be general and specific about experiences.

1 ● Write the words below in the correct column.

> a few weeks   an hour   last Tuesday
> my birthday   November   Saturday
> ten years   three days   two months   2012

For – a period of time
a few weeks

Since – a point in time

2 ●● Complete the sentences with *for* or *since*.

1 We've been here *for* nearly an hour, and the train hasn't arrived yet!
2 There has been a cinema here _____ 2002.
3 We haven't had any homework _____ Monday.
4 Mr Thomas has worked at this school _____ over twenty years.
5 Tom has been at college _____ a few months now and he loves it.
6 I've had this phone _____ last summer.

3 ●● Choose the correct option.

1 I (went)/ *have been* to New York two years ago.
2 This restaurant *opened / has opened* in 2015.
3 We *lived / have lived* in this house for two months now, so it's beginning to feel like home.
4 I *knew / have known* Paul since I was five years old – he's my best friend.
5 *Did you see / Have you seen* Emily yesterday?
6 *Did you ever go / Have you ever been* to Paris?

4 ●● Complete the dialogues with the Present Perfect or Past Simple form of the verbs in brackets.

1 A: *Have you seen* (you/see) the new James Bond film yet?
   B: Yes, I _____ (see) it last night.
2 A: I _____ (never/try) pear juice. Is it nice?
   B: Yes. I _____ (try) some last summer.
3 A: _____ (you/meet) Mark?
   B: Yes, I _____ (meet) him yesterday.
4 A: Jack _____ (not do) his Maths homework. What about you?
   B: I _____ (do) it at the weekend.

5 ●●● Complete the texts with the Present Perfect or Past Simple form of the verbs in brackets.

> I [1]*went* (go) to the Chinese restaurant in Dalton Street last night. [2]_____ (you/eat) there? The food's really nice. I [3]_____ (have) some tuna, which [4]_____ (be) very tasty!

> I [5]_____ (try) that restaurant. I [6]_____ (not like) it at all, and we [7]_____ (wait) for ages for our food! But that [8]_____ (be) about six months ago.

> I think the food [9]_____ (improve) since last year. A lot of people I know [10]_____ (enjoy) the food there. Two of my friends [11]_____ (eat) there last Saturday and they [12]_____ (not have) any complaints.

6 ●●● Complete the dialogues with one word in each gap.

A
A: [1]*Have* you ever drunk coconut milk?
B: Yes, I [2]_____. I tried it about two years ago, but I [3]_____ like it. It was disgusting! I haven't tried it again [4]_____ then.

B
A: Have you [5]_____ to the new Pizza Palace restaurant yet?
B: No, I [6]_____. Where is it?
A: It's on Clarence Street. It's been open [7]_____ about six weeks now.
B: Oh, I [8]_____ know it was there. Let's go there this evening!

I can identify specific detail in speech and describe food.

1 Complete the words for describing food.

1 sw*e*et
2 bl___d
3 b_tt_r
4 f___h
5 s__r
6 sp__y

7 r___h
8 d_y
9 d_l_c___s
10 st__e
11 t___y

2 Choose the correct option.

1 I made this cake six days ago, so it's probably a bit (stale) / spicy now.
2 I love this icing – it's bland / delicious!
3 It's a lovely sauce, but it's quite rich / tasty, so I can't eat very much.
4 Don't add too much sugar – I don't like food that's too bland / sweet.
5 These grapes are lovely and fresh / dry!
6 Lemon juice is too spicy / sour to drink.

3 🔊 09 Listen to Lily talking about the cake she has made. Mark the sentences T (true) or F (false).

1 ☐ Lily has made a cake for her friends.
2 ☐ She has made cakes since she was ten.
3 ☐ Her cake is in the shape of a boat.
4 ☐ It's a chocolate cake.
5 ☐ The filling is red.
6 ☐ You can read a message on the cake.

4 🔊 10 Listen to information about the competition Lily has entered. Complete the text.

School cake competition

Are you a champion baker? Our cake competition takes place soon. Why not make a cake and bring it along? You never know – you might win!

. . . .

Date of competition: [1]_____ June
Bring cakes to the cookery room in school before [2]_____ o'clock
Last year's winning novelty cake: a cake in the shape of an [3]_____
Cost of entry: [4]£_____ per cake
Prize: a [5]_____ and £25
Entry forms available from Mrs Cussons or the [6]_____ . . . .

5 🔊 10 Choose the correct option. Listen again and check.

1 The judges will taste the cakes before they (make) / get their decision.
2 Mrs Addison will give / announce the winner.
3 If you'd like to enter / make the competition, you need an entry form.
4 You need to write / fill in your entry form by next week.
5 Someone's going to win / earn that prize!

I can order food in a café or restaurant.

1 Match 1–6 with a–f to make sentences.

1	c	Take a seat and	a you something?
2	☐	What would you	b you are.
3	☐	Would you like	c ~~I'll get you the menu.~~
4	☐	Here	d order?
5	☐	Are you ready to	e like to drink?
6	☐	Can I get	f anything to eat?

2 Complete the sentences with the words below.

> ~~excuse~~ have please slice thanks

1 *Excuse* me, can I have some water?
2 Not for me, _____.
3 Just a smoothie for me, _____.
4 I'll _____ a coffee, please.
5 I'd like a _____ of chocolate cake, please.

3 Write the phrases below in the correct column.

> ~~Are you ready to order?~~ Can I get you something?
> Excuse me, can I have ...? Here you are.
> I'd like a ... I'll have ... Just ... for me, please.
> Not for me, thanks. What would you like to drink?
> Take a seat and I'll get you the menu.
> Would you like anything to eat?

The customer says

The waiter says
Are you ready to order?

4 Choose the correct responses.

1 Would you like anything to eat?
  a Here you are.
  ⓑ Not for me, thanks.
  c I'll get it.

2 Excuse me, can I have a strawberry smoothie, please?
  a Thanks.
  b Are you ready to order?
  c Of course.

3 Can I get you something?
  a Nearly.
  b Just a sandwich for me, please.
  c Take a seat.

4 I'd like a slice of lemon cake.
  a I'll give you the menu.
  b Me too.
  c Sorry I'm late.

5 🔊 11 Complete the dialogues with one word in each gap. Listen and check.

A

Waiter: Hello. Are you ¹*ready* to order?

Max: Yes. Can I ² _____ a banana smoothie, please?

Waiter: Of ³ _____. And would you ⁴ _____ anything to eat?

Max: No, ⁵ _____ the smoothie, please.

B

Rob: Hi! I'm sorry I'm late.

Leah: That's OK. I've just ⁶ _____ an ice cream, but the waiter hasn't brought it yet. What do you ⁷ _____?

Rob: Oh, ice cream sounds nice. Where's the waiter? Er, ⁸ _____ me, can I ⁹ _____ a vanilla ice cream, please?

Waiter: Yes, of course. Would you like anything to drink?

Rob: ¹⁰ _____ for me, thanks. Just the ice cream.

6 Complete sentences 1–3 with the words below. Then match the sentences with meanings a–c.

OUT of **class**

> fancy get guys

1 ☐ I don't _____ cake today.
2 ☐ Hi, _____.
3 ☐ It's OK. I'll _____ it.

a I can order my food and drink myself.
b I want to eat something different.
c a way of saying hello to a group of friends

I can write an email to a friend.

1 Order the letters and write the verbs in the sentences.

1 You need a knife to *chop* (hcpo) the onions and carrots.

2 _____ (ryf) the fish in a bit of butter.

3 I usually _____ (lobi) eggs for about four minutes.

4 Add the cheese and _____ (xmi) everything together.

5 _____ (liesc) the tomato and put it on top of the pizza.

2 Complete the email with the phrases below.

> ~~are things~~   can't wait   decided to have
> great to hear   I was wondering
> just finished   let me know if

From: Rob;

To: Tanya;

Hi Tanya,

How ¹*are things*? It was ²_____ from you last week. I'm really pleased that you enjoyed your holiday and I'm glad things are going well at your new school. I ³_____ to hear more about it when I see you.

We've ⁴_____ our exams here – the Maths exam was really difficult, as usual! We've ⁵_____ a class lunch to celebrate the end of the year. It's next Thursday. The plan is for everyone to make a dish and then we can all share the food. I'm making a pizza. I buy the pizza base, of course. First, I fry some onions, then I chop some tomatoes and mix those with the onions. I put that mixture onto the pizza base. I boil one or two eggs, then I slice them and put them on the pizza. Finally, I slice some cheese to put on top – delicious!

Anyway, ⁶_____ if you'd like to come. You know everyone from when you were in this class and we'd all be really pleased to see you again. Maybe you could bring a cake or some biscuits.

⁷_____ you can make it.

I hope you can!

Rob

3 Write the sentences in the correct group.

> ~~Bye for now.~~   Great to hear from you.   See you soon.
> I can't wait to hear more about it.   I'm making a pizza.
> I'm writing to ask if you'd like to come.   How are things?
> We've just finished our exams.

Starting your email	Thanks for getting in touch. _____
Responding to news	It was great to hear about your holiday.
Giving your news	We've decided to organise a class lunch. _____
Explaining why you're writing	By the way, I was wondering if you'd like to come.
Ending your email	Let me know if you can make it. *Bye for now.*

4 Complete the notes with the words below.

> at her new school   I'm making   invite her
> next Friday   suggest what she   ~~to email~~

- must remember ¹*to email* Marty (in our class last year)
- glad she's happy ²_____
- tell her about class lunch ³_____
- tell her what ⁴_____
- ⁵_____ to the lunch
- ⁶_____ should bring

5 Look at the notes in Exercise 4. Write an email to Marty. Follow the instructions below.

1 Use the email in Exercise 2 as a model.

2 Write four paragraphs:
- Paragraph 1: start your email and respond to Marty's news.
- Paragraph 2: give your news and explain why you're writing. Describe what you're making for the lunch.
- Paragraph 3: invite Marty to the class lunch.
- Paragraph 4: end your email.

3 Use cooking verbs to describe what you're making for the lunch.

3.8 SELF-ASSESSMENT

☺☺ = I understand and can help a friend. ☹ = I understand but have some questions.

☺ = I understand and can do it by myself. ☹☹ = I do not understand.

		☺☺	☺	☹	☹☹	Need help?	Now try ...
3.1	Vocabulary					Students' Book pp. 34–35 Workbook pp. 30–31	Ex. 1–2, p. 39
3.2	Grammar					Students' Book p. 36 Workbook p. 32	Ex. 3–4, p. 39
3.3	Reading					Students' Book p. 37 Workbook p. 33	
3.4	Grammar					Students' Book p. 38 Workbook p. 34	Ex. 5–6, p. 39
3.5	Listening					Students' Book p. 39 Workbook p. 35	
3.6	Speaking					Students' Book p. 40 Workbook p. 36	Ex. 7, p. 39
3.7	Writing					Students' Book p. 41 Workbook p. 37	

3.1 I can talk about food and drink.
3.2 I can use the Present Perfect with *ever, never, just, already* and *yet*.
3.3 I can find specific detail in an article and use *make* and *do* accurately.
3.4 I can talk about duration of time and be general and specific about experiences.
3.5 I can identify specific detail in speech and describe food.
3.6 I can order food in a café or restaurant.
3.7 I can write an email to a friend.

What can you remember from this unit?

New words I learned (the words you most want to remember from this unit)	**Expressions and phrases I liked** (any expressions or phrases you think sound nice, useful or funny)	**English I heard or read outside class** (e.g. from websites, books, adverts, films, music)

SELF-CHECK

1 Choose the odd one out.

1 Fruit:
garlic
grapes
pear

2 Drinks:
smoothie
cream
lemonade

3 Meat and fish:
beef
tuna
nuts

4 Sweets and snacks:
cheese
crisps
ice cream

5 Vegetables and salad:
cucumber
honey
lettuce

6 Flavours:
coconut
mint
flour

2 Choose the correct option.

1 Our school is in a modern *build / building*.
2 Jenny Sharp is the best *contestant / competition* on the show.
3 Who will *win / winner* the prize?
4 Please hurry up and *make / do* your homework!
5 I don't know what to do – I can't *make / do* a decision.
6 Don't worry about winning – just *make / do* your best.
7 Oh, I love this vanilla ice cream – it's *delicious / bland*!
8 We've got some lovely *rich / fresh* lettuce for the salad.

Grammar

3 Complete the sentences with the Present Perfect form of the verbs in brackets.

1 Don't worry, the film _____ (not start/yet).
2 _____ (you/ try/ever) chilli chocolate?
3 Come in – we _____ (finish/just) eating.
4 I _____ (see/never) Tim so angry before!
5 _____ (it/stop/raining/yet)?

4 Choose the correct answers.

1 I've _____ been to New York, but I'd love to go there one day.
   a just   b already   c never
2 James is really happy – he's _____ won a competition!
   a yet   b just   c ever
3 I haven't finished my homework_____.
   a yet   b already   c just
4 You don't need to invite Sam to the party – I've _____ invited him.
   a ever   b yet   c already

5 Complete the sentences with *for* or *since*.

1 My uncle has lived in Spain _____ two years.
2 Poor Sara has been ill _____ last Saturday.
3 There has been a school here _____ 1984.
4 I've known Sam _____ a long time.

6 Complete the sentences with the Present Perfect or Past Simple form of the verbs in brackets.

1 I _____ (visit) Paris a few times. It's a lovely city.
2 We _____ (not go) away on holiday last year.
3 Everyone _____ (enjoy) the meal last night.
4 A new café _____ (open) near our school.
5 I _____ (write) an email to Max three days ago, but he _____ (not reply) yet.
6 I _____ (never/have) a chocolate smoothie, but I _____ (try) a coconut smoothie last summer.

Speaking language practice

7 Complete the dialogues with the phrases below. There is one extra phrase.

> could I have   excuse me   nearly   of course
> thank you   would you like

1 A: Are you ready to order?
   B: _____. We'll be ready in a minute.
2 A: Can I get you something to drink?
   B: _____ a lemonade, please?
3 A: Excuse me, can I have some water, please?
   B: _____.
4 A: _____ anything to eat?
   B: Could I have a toasted sandwich, please?
5 A: Here you are.
   B: _____.

1 Match the words below with the pictures.

> BBQ ribs   chicken tikka masala   fish and chips
> ~~hot dogs~~   pepperoni pizza   sushi

1 _hot dogs_

2 _____

3 _____

4 _____

5 _____

6 _____

2 Match the foods in Exercise 1 with these countries.

- the USA   • India   • the UK   • Japan

3 Complete the sentences with the words below.

> afternoon tea   cuisines   flavours   gourmet
> ~~national dish~~   recipe   takeaway meal

1 Chicken tikka masala is now the UK's _national dish_!
2 Many British people only have a _____ for lunch.
3 Indian cuisine is full of spicy _____ .
4 A traditional British _____ is great. It has delicious cakes and sandwiches.
5 _____ burger restaurants are expensive.
6 You can try different _____ from all over the world at the Zaza Bazaar restaurant.
7 I love lots of dishes, but I don't know the _____ , so I don't know how to make them!

4 Match photos A–D with sentences 1–4. Then complete the sentences with the verbs below.

> ~~frying~~   serving   shopping for   tasting

A

B

C

D

1 [D] Lynn is _frying_ food at the market.
2 [ ] Anjum is _____ food in Liverpool.
3 [ ] Anjum is _____ food in Lynn's kitchen.
4 [ ] Anjum is _____ food in the market.

5 Make sentences in the Present Perfect.

1 Lynn / never / cook / Indian food / before
   Lynn has never cooked Indian food before.
2 she / not / make / any mistakes / yet
   _____
3 she / never / cook / outside
   _____
4 she / learn / a lot about Indian cuisine
   _____
5 they / raise / a lot of money for charity
   _____

6 Choose the correct option.

1 You can find a *total* /(wide) range of Indian food in Liverpool.
2 There's a *large* / *long* community of Keralan people there.
3 They attend a *global* / *local* farmers' market.
4 Anjum teaches Lynn three *traditional* / *modern* dishes.
5 Kerala is a *primary* / *popular* holiday destination.

7 Read the video script. Underline any words or phrases you don't know and find their meaning in your dictionary.

Indian food Liverpool style

Part 1

This is Anjum Anand. She's a food writer and a chef born in London, but of Indian origin. In this series she travels to different cities in the UK to find a wide range of Indian food and flavours. She also teaches inexperienced
5   cooks how to make great Indian food.

In this programme she's in Liverpool, where there's a large community from the Southern Indian state of Kerala. She meets Lynn Mitchell, who works for a hospital in the city. The plan is to take part in a local farmers' market to raise money for charity. Lynn wants to sell Indian food at the market. The
10   problem is that Lynn has never cooked Indian food, so it's going to be a real challenge.

Kerala is in the south-west of India and is a popular holiday destination for British people. A lot of Keralan people have come to Liverpool in the last ten years to look for work. There are now over one thousand families there.
15   Anjum is going to teach Lynn three traditional Keralan dishes – coconut chicken with ginger, which has a lovely sweet flavour, delicious salmon wraps with curry leaves and finally, rice noodles. Keralan specialities include a lot of fruit and fish. The cuisine is very light and healthy compared to other Indian food.
20   In Liverpool it's easy to find the ingredients for these dishes – Anjum can find all the fruit, vegetables and spices that she needs in special Keralan shops.

Part 2

First, Lynn chops and fries up all the ingredients. When the dishes are ready, Anjum tries them. They are really tasty! Lynn hasn't made any mistakes yet.
25   'Mmm, that's amazing!'

'Oh good, oh good!'

'That's perfect!'

'Oh fantastic!'

Now they're both ready to take the food to the market with Lynn's daughter.
30   More than 5,000 people visit Liverpool's monthly farmers' market. Indian food is very popular but the question is, will the local people like these Keralan specialities?

At first, things are not easy – people are not sure. It's the first time Lynn has ever cooked outside and she's very nervous. But then things change –
35   people seem to love the food and soon all of it has gone!

'Beautiful!'

'Mmm, tastes lovely!'

'That is excellent – but very hot!'

Since she began this project, Lynn has learnt a lot about cooking Indian food
40   and they have raised lots of money for charity. Lynn's really, really happy!

So, what do the British really eat? Keralan food – at least in Liverpool they do!

4

Curtain up!

4.1 | **VOCABULARY** | Film and TV

I can talk about films and television.

1 ● **Complete the words for types of films.**

1 com<u>ed</u>y
2 d _ _ _m_n _ _ _y
3 ac _ _ _n f_ _m
4 s _ _ -f _ _
5 f _ _ t _ _ y

6 c _ _ t _ _ n
7 f _ _ _ y t _ _ e
8 t _ _ _ll_r
9 r _ m _ _ t _ c f _ _ m

2 ●● **Read the descriptions and write the types of films. Use the words in Exercise 1.**

1 It's a beautiful love story. *romantic film*
2 It's so funny! The actors really made me laugh! _____
3 It takes place in the future, on a different planet. _____
4 It's a really interesting film about lions. _____
5 It's a traditional children's story about a princess. _____
6 The characters are drawings, not real people. _____
7 There are some amazing car chases. _____
8 It takes place in an imaginary world, where people have magic powers. _____
9 It was so exciting – I didn't know what was going to happen!
_____

3 ● **Match questions 1–4 with answers a–d.**

1 [c] What's your favourite film?
2 [ ] What's it about?
3 [ ] Who's in it?
4 [ ] What's it like?

a Daniel Craig is the main character.
b It's very exciting.
c ~~It's Spectre. It's an action film.~~
d It's about a spy.

4 ●● **Complete the dialogue with the words below.**

| about   comedy   ~~favourite~~   like   who's

A: Do you like watching films?
B: Yes, my ¹*favourite* film is *Paddington*. Some parts of it are computer generated, but some of the characters are real actors.
A: What's it ²_____?
B: It's about a bear that goes to London.
A: ³_____ in it?
B: Hugh Bonneville is Henry. He's the man who looks after Paddington.
A: What's it ⁴_____? Is it funny?
B: Yes, it's very funny. It's a brilliant ⁵_____.

5 **WORD BUILDING** Complete the table.

Verb	Noun	Person
act	[1] *action*	[2] _____
[3] _____	entertainment	entertainer
produce	[4] _____	producer
perform	performance	[5] _____

6 ●● Choose the correct option.

1 This film is great *entertain* / (*entertainment*) for all the family.
2 I think Zac Efron is a brilliant *act* / *actor*.
3 I'd love to work as a film *producer* / *production*.
4 I'd be too scared to *perform* / *performer* in front of thousands of people.
5 It isn't easy to become a successful *entertainer* / *entertain*.
6 It takes a lot of work to *production* / *produce* a film.

7 ● Match 1–8 with a–h to make sentences.

1 | d | The main character in the film
2 | | I can't wait to see the next
3 | | The show was an instant
4 | | When did the story first appear
5 | | A new sci-fi
6 | | The film has some amazing special
7 | | His first film got some great
8 | | The TV audience

a hit – everyone loved it!
b loved the show.
c reviews when it came out.
d ~~is a fifteen-year-old boy.~~
e episode in the series.
f series is starting tonight.
g effects.
h on our TV screens?

8 ●● Complete the sentences with the words below.

audience   character   episode   hit   reviews   screens
series   ~~special effects~~

1 The film uses some amazing *special effects* to give you the feeling that you are in space.
2 The show is especially popular with a young TV _____.
3 Who is your favourite _____ in the *Lord of the Rings* films?
4 The film got some bad _____ online, but I really liked it.
5 The new _____ of *X Factor* starts next week.
6 The producers were really happy that the show was such a big _____.
7 I want to get home quickly to see tonight's _____ of *The Cops*.
8 My dad is always complaining that everything on our TV _____ is rubbish!

9 ●●● Complete the text with one word in each gap.

What's on tonight?

Our reviewers give their suggestions for the best shows on TV tonight.

Hot and Cold

Channel 3, 6.30

A [1]*documentary* about how animals live in the hottest and coldest places in the world. Great [2]_____ for all the family.

Maxwell Street

BTV, 7.30

Is Kerry in danger? Don't miss this week's [3]_____ of this exciting drama [4]_____.
It isn't surprising that Maxwell Street is such a big [5]_____ – the story is great and the [6]_____, Damien Green, is brilliant as Jake, the lovable hero.

Don't call me

The Movie Channel, 8.00

If you like [7]_____ films, make sure you watch this amazing love story. Carrie Taylor gives a great [8]_____ as Emma, the main [9]_____ in the film. What's it [10]_____? Well, if want to know the story, I suggest you watch the film! It had very good [11]_____ when it first came out in cinemas and it's great to see it now on our TV [12]_____.

I can compare different things.

1 ● Complete the sentences with the comparative or superlative form of the adjectives in brackets.

1 I think the second film is _better_ (good) than the first one.

2 The _____ (funny) part was when he fell in the swimming pool.

3 I think that having a good story is _____ (important) than having famous actors.

4 These are the _____ (uncomfortable) seats I've ever sat on!

5 Going to the cinema is _____ (exciting) than watching a film at home.

6 That's the _____ (bad) film I've ever seen – it was awful!

2 ● Choose the correct answers.

1 That film was _____!
   (a) too scary   b enough scary   c as scary as

2 The main character isn't _____.
   a enough good-looking
   b good-looking enough
   c good-looking as

3 These seats aren't _____ the others.
   a as expensive as
   b expensive as
   c too expensive as

4 You're _____ to see that film.
   a too young   b enough young   c as young

5 The actors weren't _____ for me to hear.
   a too loud   b enough loud   c loud enough

6 Our TV screen is _____ yours.
   a too big as   b big enough as   c as big as

3 ●● Find and correct the mistakes in the sentences. One sentence is correct.

1 Action films are more exciting that romantic films!
   Action films are more exciting than romantic films!

2 It's funniest film I've ever seen!
   _____

3 The second part of the film was worse than the first part.
   _____

4 The seats here aren't too big as our chairs at home.
   _____

5 The music in the film was too much loud.
   _____

6 Most documentaries aren't enough interesting.
   _____

4 ●● Decide if the sentences in each pair have the same meaning (S) or a different meaning (D).

1 [D] a Jack isn't as old as his brother.
     b Jack and his brother are the same age.

2 [ ] a The new cinema is bigger than the old one.
     b The old cinema isn't as big as the new one.

3 [ ] a The tickets are too expensive.
     b The tickets are cheap enough.

4 [ ] a It's the most exciting film ever!
     b No film is as exciting as this one!

5 [ ] a These new seats are as uncomfortable as the old ones.
     b The old seats were more comfortable.

6 [ ] a It isn't warm enough.
     b It's too cold for us.

5 ●●● Complete the posts with the correct form of the adjectives in brackets.

● ● ●

Has anyone seen a 4D film? I saw one last night and it was [1] _the best_ (good) experience of my life! It was definitely much [2] _____ (exciting) a normal film.

I saw a 4D film last week, but it wasn't [3] _____ (good) I expected. The moving seats were [4] _____ (uncomfortable) for me to relax and enjoy the film.

I loved the special effects! Feeling the wind on my face during the car chase made it [5] _____ (scary) as driving fast in a real car. And the bangs on my seat when the characters were fighting were [6] _____ (realistic) to make me jump – it was great!

I tried to see a 4D film last week, but I was with my little sister and she wasn't [7] _____ (old) to watch the film. She wasn't as [8] _____ (disappointed) I was because I took her for a pizza instead!

I can understand the main points of an article and talk about entertainment.

1 Complete the sentences with the words below.

| costume   make-up   mime   puppets   ~~stage~~

1 I was really scared when I walked onto the *stage* for the first time.
2 They control the _____ by pulling strings attached to their arms and legs.
3 It takes ages to put the _____ on my face before a show.
4 The traditional _____ for women is a brightly coloured dress.
5 It's a _____ show, so the actors don't speak at all.

2 Match 1–6 with a–f to make sentences.

1 [c] Harriet wants to do
2 [ ] Sam told us
3 [ ] Would you like to watch
4 [ ] The film got
5 [ ] She'd love to star
6 [ ] I'm too shy to go

a very good reviews.   d on stage.
b in a film.   e the show with us?
c ~~a dance workshop.~~   f an amazing story.

3 Read the texts and the reviews. Match each person with the best play for them. There is one extra review.

Noah [ ]

I'm not into classic theatre. I prefer smaller theatres and modern plays, which deal with important issues that are relevant today. I'm not particularly interested in seeing well-known actors – I can see them on TV any time. I prefer to see young actors.

Beth [ ]

I prefer traditional theatre, especially plays by the great writers like Shakespeare. I love seeing famous actors who really know how to act well. I enjoy both big and small theatres, and my favourite is open air theatre.

Anna [ ]

I'm not keen on small theatres and serious plays. I love the excitement of a really big theatre and I'm a big fan of musicals. I especially love shows with well-known singers in them.

A The Fall of Rome

Stanley Ibotson is excellent in this new adaptation of this classic eighteenth century drama. The production has won praise from both audiences and critics, and the outdoor setting of Graymore Hall is perfect for the dramatic battle scenes. There are some wonderful performances, especially by Ibotson, who is returning to live theatre after two years in TV dramas.

B The Heat is On

The Heat is On is a thought-provoking new play which imagines a world where climate change has run out of control. At only nineteen years old, Sophie Johnson gives a brilliant performance as the main character, Eve, who struggles to cope with life in a world where global warming is a reality.

C The Traffic Cops

This is slapstick comedy at its best! It was voted Best New Comedy earlier this year, and has delighted audiences up and down the country. First shown in Sheffield, it has now moved to the Royal Theatre, one of the biggest theatres in the West End. A great success for young writer Tom Clancy, and definitely worth seeing!

D Don't Stop Dancing!

Celine is definitely a big hit in this spectacular show at the Abbey Theatre. The show is full of colour, with beautiful costumes, great music and some amazing dance routines. Celine's decision to develop a career in the theatre after the break-up of her band disappointed some of her fans, but she's certainly winning over plenty of new ones now. Don't miss it!

I can talk about quantities of countable and uncountable nouns.

1 ● Write the quantifiers in the correct column.

| (a) few (a) little a lot of any lots of many much some

Countable nouns	Uncountable nouns	Countable and uncountable nouns
a few		

2 ● Choose the correct option.

1 How *much* / *many* cousins have you got?
2 How *much* / *many* food do we need?
3 I've got *some* / *any* new jeans.
4 She doesn't have *some* / *any* jewellery.
5 Are there *some* / *any* festivals in your town?
6 Tara has got *a little* / *a lot* of friends.

3 ● Match 1–4 with a–d to make sentences.

1 [c] Can you wait a few
2 [ ] Hurry up – we've got very little
3 [ ] There are very few
4 [ ] I can lend you a little

a time before the show starts.
b money if you like.
c ~~minutes? I'm nearly ready.~~
d festivals in this area – only one or two.

4 ●● Read the dialogue. Choose the correct answers.

A: Hi, Lottie. Would you like to see [1]_____ photos of the Notting Hill Carnival?
B: Oh yes, please. Is it a big carnival? How [2]_____ people take part in it?
A: [3]_____ people! Look, that's me, wearing my traditional costume.
B: Wow! It's colourful. Do you play in a band?
A: Yes, I've got [4]_____ really nice photos of the band – look.
B: It must be great fun to play in front of all those people.
A: Yes, but it's also a bit stressful. We had very [5]_____ time to practise this year, so I was a bit nervous.
B: Did you make [6]_____ mistakes on the day?
A: Actually, we made very [7]_____ mistakes – I was really pleased.

1	ⓐ some	b any	c few	d lots
2	a lots of	b a lot of	c many	d much
3	a Much	b A little	c Lots	d Lots of
4	a few	b a few	c any	d much
5	a little	b a little	c few	d a few
6	a much	b few	c any	d lots
7	a little	b few	c many	d a few

5 ●●● Complete the email with one word in each gap.

From: Anita;
To: Lottie;

Hi Lottie,

Do you want to come and celebrate Diwali with me and my family next week? My mum says I can invite a [1]*few* friends and, of course, all my cousins will be there – there are lots [2]_____ them, so it should be fun! There's a really big celebration here in Leicester.

You can wear what you want. You don't have to wear [3]_____ special clothes. Not very [4]_____ of my friends wear traditional clothes, which I think is a pity. Bring [5]_____ warm clothes, though, because we always go out into the streets to celebrate and set off fireworks. You should probably bring a [6]_____ money too because there are a [7]_____ of lovely traditional foods you can buy in the streets.

I hope you can come! I always get really excited about Diwali, and there isn't [8]_____ time to wait now – just a few more days!
See you soon, I hope!
Anita

6 Match questions 1–3 with answers a–c.

OUT of **class**

1 [ ] How long does it take to put your costume on?
2 [ ] How many people come to the festival?
3 [ ] How do you fix the flowers in your hair?

a Lots. b Like this. c Ages.

I can identify specific detail in speech and talk about festivals.

1 Match 1–5 with a–e to make sentences.

1. ☐ d ☐ The festival celebrates all aspects of country
2. ☐ We really enjoyed our summer
3. ☐ I love carnival
4. ☐ Everyone had a piece of my birthday
5. ☐ I'm going to wear my new party

a. cake – it was delicious!
b. dress on Saturday.
c. vacation in Mexico.
d. ~~life~~.
e. music and all the colourful costumes.

2 Complete the sentences with compound nouns using one word from each list below.

| country family straw ~~square~~ summer |

| clothes ~~dance~~ hat party music |

1. Some people got up to do a _square dance_ when the music started.
2. Last winter we organised a big _____ to celebrate my granddad's birthday. About fifty of my relations were there.
3. It's very hot in Spain, so bring plenty of _____ with you when you come to visit.
4. It was a hot day and Lily was wearing a _____ on her head.
5. I love dancing to _____. Everyone can join in!

3 🔊 12 Listen to part of a radio programme. Tick (✓) the events that are taking place during the festival.

1. ☐ dance workshops
2. ☐ drama workshops
3. ☐ live performances
4. ☐ talks by actors
5. ☐ opportunities to perform on stage
6. ☐ theatre make-up workshops

4 🔊 13 Listen to Max and Jess talking about the festival. Choose the correct answers.

1. Why did Jess take part in this workshop?
   a. Her teacher recommended it.
   b. Her friend Rosie invited her.
   c. She enjoyed a drama lesson at school.
2. What did she learn about mime?
   a. You use your face and your body to show your feelings.
   b. It's best if you show your real feelings.
   c. You have to show feelings very strongly.
3. What happened at lunchtime?
   a. Jess felt ill.
   b. A girl had an accident.
   c. The teacher decided to play the main character.
4. What problem was there in the final show?
   a. The music was too loud.
   b. Some of the actors forgot their costumes.
   c. The lights didn't work properly.
5. What did Jess enjoy the most?
   a. The final show.
   b. Learning some dance moves.
   c. Meeting new people.

5 🔊 13 Complete the sentences with the words in the box. Listen again and check.

| artists lights moves teacher workshops |

1. Rosie is always inviting me to go to drama _____ with her.
2. We've got this new drama _____ at school.
3. The make-up _____ did a great job.
4. The only thing that went wrong was the stage _____.
5. They taught us some really good dance _____.

I can ask about, express and explain preferences.

1 Order the words to make sentences.

1 you / rather / on / Saturday / what / do / would / ?

What would you rather do on Saturday?

2 prefer / go / to / I'd / shopping

_____

3 film / this / very / sounds / funny

_____

4 you / where / go / would / rather / on holiday / ?

_____

5 tonight / prefer / what / do / to / you / would / ?

_____

6 rather / I'd / film / at home / watch / a

_____

2 Complete the sentences with the words below. There is one extra word.

| do   look (x2)   rather   prefer   sounds   would

1 Mmm, those pizzas *look* good.
2 There are two comedies on. Which one would you _____ to go to?
3 I'd _____ have something to eat first and then go to the cinema.
4 The puppet show _____ boring!
5 Which event _____ you prefer to go to this afternoon?
6 All the shows _____ great – it's difficult to choose.

3 Choose the correct responses.

1 How was the music workshop?
   a I'd prefer to do the dance workshop.
   (b) Great! I loved it!
   c What would you rather do?

2 I'd rather see the puppet show.
   a How was it?
   b What would you prefer to see?
   c OK. Cool! Let's do that.

3 Where would you rather eat?
   a I'd prefer a pizza restaurant.
   b No, thanks.
   c OK. Cool!

4 I'd prefer to go to the singing workshop.
   a Definitely the comedy workshop.
   b Yeah, it sounds great.
   c Why not?

4 🔊 14 Complete the dialogue with sentences a–g. There is one extra sentence. Listen and check.

Mark: This is a great festival, isn't it?

Tamsin: Yeah, there are so many good workshops. ¹*d*

Mark: It was really good. I definitely want to spend more time playing my guitar.

Tamsin: So, let's see what's on this afternoon. Oh, there's a hip hop dance workshop. ² _____ I'd like to try that!

Mark: I'm not sure. ³ _____ And I don't really like hip hop!

Tamsin: OK. Let's see what else there is. ⁴ _____ Do you want to do another workshop?

Mark: ⁵ _____ Are there any concerts on?

Tamsin: Yes, there's a rock band playing at two o'clock.

Mark: OK, why don't we go and watch the band and then get something to eat after that?

Tamsin: ⁶ _____ I'm really hungry!

Mark: OK. Cool! Let's do that. There are some really nice-looking burgers over there!

a That sounds fun.
b What would you rather do?
c I'd rather have something to eat now.
d How was the music workshop?
e I'm not into rock music.
f I'd prefer to listen to some music.
g I'm not mad about dancing.

5 Order the words in a–b to make sentences. Then use the sentences to complete dialogues 1–2.

OUT of class

a singing / mad / I'm / about / not

_____

b sounds / interesting / it / really

_____

1 A: Do you want to go to that talk about animals in the theatre?
   B: Yeah. _____

2 A: There's a choir workshop on later. Do you want to try it?
   B: No. _____

I can describe how people do things.

1 Write the adverbs.

1 clear – *clearly*
2 loud – _____
3 safe – _____
4 happy – _____
5 good – _____
6 straight – _____
7 angry – _____
8 early – _____

2 Complete the sentences with adverbs formed from the adjectives below.

careful fast hard late loud patient

1 Carry the drink **carefully** so you don't spill it.
2 Everyone else was there at eight o'clock, but Sam arrived _____, as usual!
3 My leg hurts, so I can't walk very _____.
4 Make sure you speak _____ so that everyone can hear you.
5 My parents are always telling me that I should work _____ at school.
6 They waited _____ for over three hours!

3 Choose the correct option.

1 We (finished the job quickly)/ finished quickly the job and went home.
2 Dana *sings beautifully / beautifully sings* and she can dance too.
3 He walked out and *shut angrily the door / shut the door angrily*.
4 Please *speak clearly / clearly speak*.
5 He always *loudly plays music / plays music loudly* when he's at home.
6 Why do you always *slowly walk / walk slowly*?

4 Complete the sentences with the comparative or superlative form of the adverbs in brackets.

1 My brother works *harder* (hard) than me at school.
2 Kevin arrived _____ (early) than everyone else.
3 My mum drives _____ (safely) than my dad.
4 They all had a competition to see who could run _____ (fast).
5 Do children here behave _____ (politely) than in other countries?
6 Everyone in our class works hard, but Dan works _____ (hard).

5 Complete the second sentence so that it means the same as the first sentence. Use no more than three words.

1 Serena is a very fast eater at meal times.
Serena *eats very fast* at meal times.
2 No one in our class can swim faster than George.
George can _____ in our class.
3 In your exam, please be polite when you answer the questions.
In your exam, please answer _____.
4 Don't go anywhere else on your way home.
Go _____ home.
5 Mike didn't arrive on time, as usual!
Mike arrived _____, as usual!
6 Let's be patient while we wait for the others.
Let's _____ for the others.

6 Read the email. Choose the correct answers.

| From: | Ellie; |
| To: | Libby; |

Hi Libby,
I did a circus skills course last week. It was ¹_____ fun! First, we tried juggling with three balls, and I learned that quite ²_____. In fact, everything was going very ³_____ until I tried riding the unicycle – you know, the bike with only one wheel. I think I fell off so many times because I was trying to ride ⁴_____ than everyone else. It seems that if you ride a bit ⁵_____, it's easier to stay on. Anyway, I'm now in hospital with a broken ankle, so I guess I'll just have to wait ⁶_____ until I'm better!
Come and see me soon!
Ellie

1 **a** great
  b greatly
  c greatest
  d the most greatly
2 **a** quick
  b quickly
  c quicker
  d more quickly
3 **a** good
  b better
  c well
  d best
4 **a** slow
  b slowly
  c the slowest
  d more slowly
5 **a** quick
  b faster
  c safe
  d more careless
6 **a** patient
  b patiently
  c more patient
  d most patiently

4.8 SELF-ASSESSMENT

For each learning objective, tick (✓) the box that best matches your ability.

☺☺ = I understand and can help a friend.　☹ = I understand but have some questions.

☺ = I understand and can do it by myself.　☹☹ = I do not understand.

		☺☺	☺	☹	☹☹	Need help?	Now try ...
4.1	Vocabulary					Students' Book pp. 46–47 Workbook pp. 42–43	Ex. 1–2, p. 51
4.2	Grammar					Students' Book p. 48 Workbook p. 44	Ex. 3, p. 51
4.3	Reading					Students' Book p. 49 Workbook p. 45	
4.4	Grammar					Students' Book p. 50 Workbook p. 46	Ex. 4, p. 51
4.5	Listening					Students' Book p. 51 Workbook p. 47	
4.6	Speaking					Students' Book p. 52 Workbook p. 48	Ex. 6, p. 51
4.7	English in Use					Students' Book p. 53 Workbook p. 49	Ex. 5, p. 51

4.1　I can talk about films and television.
4.2　I can compare different things.
4.3　I can understand the main points of an article and talk about entertainment.
4.4　I can talk about quantities of countable and uncountable nouns.
4.5　I can identify specific detail in speech and talk about festivals.
4.6　I can ask about, express and explain preferences.
4.7　I can describe how people do things.

What can you remember from this unit?

New words I learned (the words you most want to remember from this unit)	Expressions and phrases I liked (any expressions or phrases you think sound nice, useful or funny)	English I heard or read outside class (e.g. from websites, books, adverts, films, music)

Vocabulary

1 Complete the words in the sentences.

1 We watched a brilliant **s**_ _ - _ _ _ film about people building a city on Mars.

2 *Ratatouille* is a **c**_ _ _ _ _ _ _. The characters are drawings, not real people.

3 All the reviewers agree that she gave a very good **p**_ _ _ _ _ _ _ _ _ _ in the film.

4 Who plays the main **c**_ _ _ _ _ _ _ _ in the film?

5 The show was a big **h**_ _ _ with the people in Britain and the USA.

6 The **a**_ _ _ _ _ _ _ _ clapped loudly at the end of the show.

2 Complete the sentences with the words below.

| cake dance life party toilet vacation

1 I'm looking forward to lying on the beach in my summer _____.

2 Don't forget to buy some _____ paper for the bathroom.

3 You can do a square _____ to this music.

4 He doesn't enjoy country _____ and can't wait to move to the city!

5 You look lovely in your _____ dress!

6 I've never tried corn _____, but it sounds delicious.

Grammar

3 Complete the second sentence so that it means the same as the first sentence. Use no more than three words.

1 Documentaries aren't as popular as comedies.
Comedies are _____ documentaries.

2 The seats in the theatre weren't big enough.
The seats in the theatre _____ small.

3 No one in our class is as tall as Paul.
Paul is _____ in our class.

4 The seats at the front are more expensive than the seats at the back.
The seats at the back aren't _____ the seats at the front.

5 I've never seen a better play than this one.
This is _____ I've ever seen.

6 You're too young to go to the cinema on your own.
You aren't _____ go to the cinema on your own.

4 Choose the correct option.

1 How *much / many* people went on the school theatre trip?

2 Jake's got *many / lots of* money!

3 I'm sorry I haven't got *some / any* apple juice.

4 There isn't *much / many* food left.

5 I've seen a *few / little* good films this year.

6 My dad gets very *a few / little* time off work.

5 Complete the sentences with adverbs formed from the adjectives below.

| angry early fast good late quiet

1 That was a great show – everyone performed very _____!

2 The show starts at seven, but we need to get there _____ to get good seats.

3 I closed the door _____ because I didn't want to make a noise and wake the baby.

4 'Why did you take my money?' he shouted _____.

5 I was running as _____ as I could, but I couldn't keep up with her.

6 I arrived at the station _____ and missed my train.

Speaking language practice

6 Complete the dialogues with the phrases below.

| it sounds   I'd prefer   I'd rather   very scary
where would you rather   which would you prefer

A

A: Shall we go to the cinema tonight?

B: ¹_____ stay in and watch a film at home.

A: OK. Shall we watch that new comedy?

B: Yeah, ²_____ very funny.

B

A: There's a pizza restaurant on Broad Street or the burger bar on New Road.
³_____ go?

B: ⁴_____ to go for a pizza.

A: OK. Cool! Let's go there.

C

A: There's a musical on at the Key Theatre or a thriller at the Lady Anne Theatre.
⁵_____ to see?

B: Definitely the thriller! It looks ⁶_____!

1 Match words 1–5 with words a–e to make word friends from the text. How many other word friends can you make?

1 [c] traditional   **a** atmosphere
2 [ ] military   **b** calendar
3 [ ] annual   **c** ~~festivities~~
4 [ ] cultural   **d** parade
5 [ ] great   **e** events

2 Complete the sentences with the word friends in Exercise 1.

1 [ ] There is a mix of *traditional festivities* and modern ones where I live. I prefer the modern ones.
2 [ ] There's a _____ on New Year's Eve. Everybody has a great time.
3 [ ] There are only a few important festivals in the _____ – two or three days out of 365.
4 [ ] There isn't a _____ where I live because there isn't an army base nearby.
5 [ ] The best _____ in my town are music concerts and art exhibitions.

3 Tick (✓) the sentences in Exercise 2 that are true about where you live. Change the other sentences to make them true.

4 Choose the correct option.

1 The Trooping of the Colour (celebrates) / parades the Queen's Birthday.
2 They *welcome* / *hold* the Notting Hill Carnival in London.
3 The Chinese New Year *mentions* / *highlights* Chinese culture.
4 One of the great things about Diwali is *sensing* / *tasting* traditional Indian food.

5 Match the word friends below with the photos.

> British weather   ~~colourful costumes~~   delicious food
> happy crowd   live entertainment

1   *colourful costumes*   2 _____

3 _____   4 _____

5 _____

6 Make sentences from the video using comparatives and superlatives.

1 it's / large / Chinese New Year celebration outside China
It's the largest Chinese New Year celebration outside China.
2 the Notting Hill Carnival is / big / street festival in Europe
_____
3 today the festival is / safe / than / it was in the past
_____
4 the Notting Hill Carnival is a / loud / celebration / than / the Chinese New Year
_____

7 Choose the correct option.

1 A (melting) / *meeting* pot of cultures, London is quite unique.
2 It's a *great* / *large* opportunity for Chinese businesses to make some money.
3 Many people come to the party over the *festive* / *fun* weekend.
4 People are coming together to forget their *troubles* / *tricks*.
5 When the party is over, the *big* / *small* clean-up begins.

8 Read the video script. Underline any words or phrases you don't know and find their meaning in your dictionary.

London celebrates

Part 1

Narrator: A melting pot of cultures, London is quite unique. Now it's February, the usual time to celebrate Chinese New Year. This year is the Year of the Horse. The entertainment certainly is impressive, so it's a great tourist
5 attraction.

Man: I'm from Shanghai, China. We are visitors here and we happen to be here. It's a quite exciting place.

Woman: It's getting better and better, and it has got a Western touch which makes it very unique.

10 Narrator: This is the largest Chinese New Year Celebration that London has ever seen. It's also the largest celebration outside China with tens of thousands of people here in Central London. It's a great opportunity for Chinese businesses to make some money. With Chinatown just next door to the celebrations in London's Trafalgar Square, you can enjoy a complete
15 Chinese experience. There is lots of singing and dancing here, as well as the delicious food in Soho. As the Chinese say: 'Happy New Year!'

Part 2

Narrator: For a louder experience, come to the capital at the end of August to see Londoners celebrating the Notting Hill Carnival. So, why is it so
20 special?

Woman: The food, the music, the vibes … the rain can't stop us. Let's face it.

Woman: It's just the atmosphere – it's so friendly. Everybody's having such a fantastic time.

Man: It's part of the culture. We're here to celebrate that culture. We're here to
25 celebrate our people.

Narrator: For fifty years, people have celebrated UK Caribbean culture with all of the features that make Carnival so unique. There are colourful costumes, great live music performances and lots of partying in the streets. Even the typical British summer weather – light rain and a few clouds – can't
30 stop these people having a good time! It's now the biggest street festival in Europe, with more than a million people coming to the party over the festive weekend – both tourists and locals.

People: Welcome to the final day of the Notting Hill Carnival!

Narrator: These are steel pan instruments from the West Indies. But you can expect
35 modern dance music and a great diversity in the crowd too. In fact, there are people of all ages here, coming together to forget their troubles and have a great time!

To make sure everyone is safe, there are 7,000 police officers here to patrol the event. But today the festival is much safer than it was. It's a
40 shame that it's only two days long. When the party is over on Sunday night, the big clean-up begins!

The big match!

I can talk about sports and sports events.

1 ● Look at the pictures and complete the words.

1 b a d m i n t o n   2 i _ _ - s _ _ _ _ _   3 g _ _ _ _ _ _ _ _

4 d _ _ _ _ _   5 s _ _ _ _ _ _ _ _ _ _   6 v _ _ _ _ _ _ _ _

7 h _ _ _ _ _ _   8 s _ _ _ _ _

2 ●● Read the descriptions. Write the sports.

1 It's a really exciting sport. You use a paddle to move through the water. *kayaking*

2 This is a very relaxing sport. You move your body slowly into different positions. It's good for stretching your muscles.

_____

3 I play this sport for my school team. You can throw the ball to other people or you can run and bounce the ball on the ground. You score points by throwing the ball through a hoop. _____

4 You need to be strong to do this sport. You use your arms to pull yourself up the side of a mountain. _____

5 The ball you use for this sport is very small. You hit it across a table. _____

6 I love animals, so this is my favourite sport. You have to wear a special hat to protect your head if you fall off. _____

3 ● **WORD FRIENDS** Match 1–5 with a–e to make sentences.

1 | d | I sometimes go   a karate – he loves
2 | ☐ | I've decided to   martial arts!
        take   b volleyball at school.
3 | ☐ | My brother does   c up gymnastics.
4 | ☐ | I have skiing   d ~~walking with my~~
5 | ☐ | I sometimes   ~~friends.~~
        play   e lessons in the winter.

4 ●● Choose the correct words to complete the sentences.

1 Would you like to *play / do* yoga?
2 I want to *take / get* up a new sport this year.
3 A lot of my friends *go / play* skiing in the winter.
4 Do you *have / do* a tennis lesson every week?
5 I sometimes *go / play* handball with my friends.
6 You need to be very fit to *do / play* gymnastics.

5 ● Complete the words in the sentences.

1 We get changed in the **ch**a n g i n g **ro**o m s before the game.
2 Our team wears a blue and white **k**_ _ _.
3 I'd love to be a team **m**_ _ _ _ _**t** and walk onto the pitch with the players.
4 There were over 50,000 people in the **s**_ _ _ _ _ _**m** for the big match.
5 Our **s**_ _ _ _**s** were right at the front, so we could see the players really well.
6 At the end of the game, the **s**_ _ _ _ _ **b**_ _ _**d** said 12–8 to my team!

6 ●● Complete the dialogue with the words below. There is one extra word.

▌ fans   goal   kit   ~~match~~   pitch   score   team

A: Wow! That was a really exciting football ¹*match*! I'm glad our ²_____ won in the end.
B: Yes. I was a bit worried at half time when the ³_____ was 1–0 to the other team, but then Juan Fernandez scored that amazing ⁴_____!
A: Yes. That gave our players a lot of confidence. And the ⁵_____ all got really excited when he scored another one!
B: Yeah. A few people tried to run onto the ⁶_____ to celebrate, but of course, you aren't allowed to do that!

7 ●●● Complete the email with one word in each gap.

From: Gary;
To: Polly;

Hi Polly,

I can't believe I'm here at the Olympic Games! On Tuesday we watched the ¹*table* tennis. It's amazing how hard they hit the ball at each other across the table! Then we had tickets to watch the ²_____. I can't believe how high up they are before they drop down into the water! Our ³_____ were quite close to the pool, so we got a good view. It looks really scary, so it isn't a sport I ever want to ⁴_____ up.

On Wednesday we saw a bit of karate. It looks like a really fun sport. A few of my friends ⁵_____ karate already, so I might ask them where they ⁶_____ lessons. Maybe I'll go along with them.

Yesterday we watched some ⁷_____ matches. The players are amazing – the way they run, bouncing the ball on the ground – and they can throw it into the net from the halfway line! I was supporting the ⁸_____ from the USA. I can't remember what the final ⁹_____ was, but I know the USA won quite easily. It was great being part of a big crowd of sports ¹⁰_____.
We all cheered when one of our players ¹¹_____ some more points.

Anyway, I definitely want to do more sport when I get back home on Friday. Let's ¹²_____ swimming on Saturday!

Gary

I can talk about plans, predictions, arrangements and timetables.

1 ● Match the verbs in bold in sentences 1–6 with functions a–f.

1 [c] Off you go. I'm sure you**'ll have** fun.
2 [ ] Don't worry, I**'ll do** the washing up.
3 [ ] I**'m meeting** Sam this afternoon.
4 [ ] I**'m going to get** fit this year!
5 [ ] Look – it**'s going to rain**.
6 [ ] The film **starts** at 7.30.

a an arrangement
b a timetable
c ~~a prediction made at the moment of speaking~~
d a prediction based on what we know now
e a decision made at the moment of speaking
f a plan

2 ● Choose the correct option.

1 They're a very good team – I think (they'll win)/ they win today.
2 Hurry up – the train *leaves* / *will leave* in fifteen minutes!
3 Is your bag heavy? Wait, *I help* / *I'll help* you.
4 *I'll go* / *I'm going* on holiday on Saturday.
5 Freddie *will join* / *is going to join* a gym so he can do more training.
6 Be careful on that ladder – *you're going to fall* / *you fall*.

3 ●● Read the dialogue. Choose the correct answers.

A: Hi, James. What are your plans for the weekend?
B: Well, I ¹_____ football on Saturday afternoon.
A: Really? What time ²_____ the game start?
B: At three o'clock.
A: Cool! ³_____ and watch.
B: Great! I think it ⁴_____ an exciting game.
A: Good. What about later? Have you got any plans?
B: Yes, Ali ⁵_____ me after the game. He wants to go to the cinema in the evening. Do you want to come with us?
A: Sorry, I can't. ⁶_____ dinner with my grandparents at eight o'clock. Maybe next week.

1 a I play   (b) I'm playing   c I going to play
2 a will   b is   c does
3 a I'll come   b I come   c I'm coming
4 a is   b will be   c is being
5 a calls   b is going to call c won't call
6 a I'm having   b I'll have   c I have

4 ●● Complete the second sentence so that it means the same as the first sentence. Use no more than three words.

1 Nick's plan is to get a part-time job.
   Nick *is going to* get part-time job.
2 What's the closing time at the gym?
   What time _____ close?
3 What's your prediction for the final score?
   What do you think the final score _____?
4 What time is your meeting with the head teacher?
   What time are _____ the head teacher?

5 ●●● Choose the correct option.

MESSAGES

Hi. Mia ¹*comes* / *is coming* round to my house this evening to watch a film. Do you want to come?

What film ²*will you* / *are you going* to watch?

The new James Bond film. I think you ³*enjoy* / *'ll enjoy* it.

OK. My tennis lesson ⁴*finishes* / *will finish* at 5.30, so I can come after that.

Great! Mia ⁵*is going to order* / *orders* some pizzas too – well, that's the plan. I need to remind her!

Cool! And ⁶*I'm going to bring* / *I'll bring* some snacks with me.

Great! See you later.

OUT of class

6 Complete the sentences with the words below.

| doesn't take   important thing   let me

1 _____ have a quick go.
2 The _____ is to keep your back straight.
3 It _____ long to build up your strength.

I can identify specific detail in an article and talk about volunteering at a sports event.

1 Choose the correct option.

1 We were trying to get to Manchester, but we *ended up / set up* in London!

2 Will you help me *pick up / tidy up* the kitchen?

3 Jack had to *give up / end up* football when he hurt his knee.

4 I'd love to *take up / set up* a gymnastics club at school.

5 My uncle offered to *pick me up / set me up* from the airport.

6 I wanted to get fit, so I decided to *pick up / take up* running.

2 Read the article. Complete the form.

> Name: George Samson   Age: 16
>
> Start date of the event: ¹_____
>
> No. of days attending the event: ²_____
>
> - Access allowed to sports halls and
>   ³_____
> - Photography allowed, but no ⁴_____
> - Interview rooms available from 10 a.m.
>   till ⁵_____
> - Lunch available in the ⁶_____

3 Read the article again. Mark the sentences T (true) or F (false).

1 ☐ George writes articles for a local newspaper.

2 ☐ He has not worked as an official press reporter before.

3 ☐ The sports event lasts for three days.

4 ☐ George isn't going to take many photos.

5 ☐ He won't have to pay for food at the event.

6 ☐ You can find details of the event in the school magazine.

4 Find the phrasal verbs below in the article. Then use them to complete the sentences.

| check out   hang out   ~~help out~~   look out for   miss out

1 I've volunteered to *help out* at a festival in my town next summer.

2 I meet my friends after school and we _____ in the park together.

3 Of course I'm going to Jo's party – I don't want to _____ on all the fun!

4 You should _____ the new pizza restaurant in town – it's really good!

5 I really want to see this film – I'll _____ it at my local cinema.

My name's George Samson and I'm sixteen. I often write articles for the school magazine because I want to be a journalist when I leave school. Next week I'm going on my first trip as an official press reporter. I'm attending a sports event for disabled teenagers and I'm really looking forward to it.

The event starts on Friday 14 May and goes on for four days. I've only got entry for the Saturday and Sunday, but I'm sure there will be lots to see. I don't want to miss out on any of the excitement! As a young journalist, I can go into all the sports halls and also the swimming pool. I'm going to take my camera, of course, and I'm allowed to take as many photos as I like – I'll probably take loads! Videos aren't allowed though. There are special interview rooms where I can talk to some of the competitors. They're only open from ten in the morning until two in the afternoon, so I'll have to be well organised! There's also a special food tent where all the journalists can get free food at lunch time, so I'll be able to hang out with some professional journalists!

If you love sport, why not come along to the event? You can help out as a volunteer if you want. Check out the website for more details and look out for my report in next month's magazine!

I can talk about possible future situations.

1 ● **Choose the correct option.**

1 *You enjoy /* You'll enjoy *gymnastics if you try / you'll try it.*

2 *If you have / you'll have* some skiing lessons, *you be / you'll be* a very good skier.

3 We *don't go / won't go* walking unless the weather *is / will be* good.

4 *You get / You'll get* fitter if *you join / you'll join* a gym.

5 *I call / I'll call* you when *I get / I'll get* home.

6 You *don't improve / won't improve* unless *you practise / you'll practise*.

2 ● **Complete the sentences with *if* or *unless*.**

1 We'll go to the match <u>unless</u> the tickets are too expensive.

2 He won't lose weight _____ he doesn't do any exercise.

3 You won't get into the team _____ you're very good.

4 We'll stop playing _____ it starts to rain.

5 They won't cancel the game _____ the weather is so bad that they can't play.

6 They won't let you in _____ you don't have a ticket.

3 ●● **Complete the dialogue with the correct form of the verbs in brackets.**

A: Do you want to come ice skating with me on Saturday?

B: Er, I haven't got any skates.

A: I'm sure Jenna ¹<u>will lend</u> (lend) you hers if you ² _____ (ask) her.

B: But I'm worried I ³ _____ (hurt) myself if I ⁴ _____ (fall) over.

A: Don't worry. You ⁵ _____ (not get) injured if you ⁶ _____ (be) careful.

B: But sometimes there are loads of people there.

A: Well, if it ⁷ _____ (be) very busy when we get there, we ⁸ _____ (wait) until it's quieter. We ⁹ _____ (not go) on the ice unless you ¹⁰ _____ (feel) it's safe.

B: OK. Why not? I'll give it a go!

4 ●● **Complete the second sentence so that it means the same as the first sentence. Use no more than three words.**

1 We won't go climbing unless it's sunny.
We <u>will go</u> climbing if it's sunny.

2 I'll pay for lunch if it isn't too expensive.
I'll pay for lunch _____ is too expensive.

3 Our holiday won't be fun if the weather isn't good.
Our holiday will be fun _____ is good.

4 You won't become a great footballer unless you practise every day.
You won't become a great footballer if _____ practise every day.

5 We'll be there at three o'clock if our train is on time.
We'll be there at three o'clock _____ is late.

6 I'll play tennis on Saturday unless I'm still ill.
I'll play tennis on Saturday _____ better.

5 ●●● **Read the text. Choose the correct answers.**

So, my climbing adventure starts today! I've got my first lesson at the Climbing Centre in my town. I'm feeling a bit nervous, but I know that the instructors will help me ¹ _____ have any problems. I'll start on the junior climbing wall and I'll have a rope on, so I won't get hurt ² _____ fall. There are three higher walls, but the instructors probably won't allow me to go on them ³ _____ think I'm able to cope with them. My uncle does loads of climbing and he says that ⁴ _____ enjoy it, he'll take me climbing with him in the mountains. I won't go with him ⁵ _____ feel really confident though. Climbing can be a dangerous sport!

Well, I must go now. My lesson starts at two and I'll be late ⁶ _____ leave soon!

1 a if I'll   c unless I
  b if I   d if I don't

2 a if I   c unless I
  b if I'll   d if I won't

3 a unless they'll   c if they
  b unless they   d if they won't

4 a unless I   c if I won't
  b if I'll   d if I

5 a if I won't   c if I'll
  b unless I'll   d unless I

6 a if I   c unless I
  b if I won't   d unless I'll

I can identify specific detail in speech and talk about sports training.

1 WORD BUILDING **Complete the table.**

Verb	Noun (action)	Noun (person)
¹*train*	training	² _____
run	³ _____	runner
play	–	⁴ _____
⁵ _____	practice	–
coach	–	⁶ _____
⁷ _____	race	racer
score	⁸ _____	scorer
⁹ _____	kick	–

2 Complete the sentences with a word formed from the word in brackets.

1 They do three hours of *training* (train) every week.
2 Rob _____ (practice) his football skills every day.
3 Stella is a really good tennis _____ (play).
4 All the _____ (run) looked exhausted at the end of the race.
5 My uncle works as a sports _____ (train).
6 Who _____ (score) the winning goal in last week's match?

3 🔊 **15 Listen to a sports report. Choose the correct answers.**

1 What does Anita most enjoy doing in tennis?

A B C

2 What form of training does Anita do every day?

A B C

3 Who always watches Anita's matches?

A B C

4 What does Anita always wear when she plays matches?

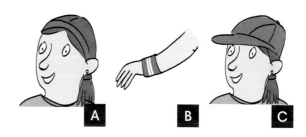

A B C

4 🔊 **16 Listen to Angela and Paul talking about Anita Redway. Mark the sentences T (true) or F (false).**

1 ☐ Angela is surprised that Anita is going to give up playing tennis.
2 ☐ Paul thinks it's better for Anita to focus on doing something that she enjoys.
3 ☐ Anita already has a lot of other interests.
4 ☐ Angela thinks Anita will earn a lot of money from coaching.
5 ☐ Paul and Angela agree that Anita will be a popular coach.
6 ☐ Anita's ambition is to help another player to achieve success.

I can ask and talk about plans.

1 Match 1–6 with a–f to make sentences.

1 [c] What are you up
2 [ ] I don't have
3 [ ] Have you got any
4 [ ] I'm visiting my
5 [ ] What are you
6 [ ] I'm going to

a doing tonight?
b grandparents on Sunday.
c ~~to on Saturday?~~
d the cinema on Friday.
e any plans yet.
f plans for the weekend?

2 Complete the dialogue with the words below.

| about after ~~first~~ know then what |

A: What are you doing at the weekend, Laura?

B: ¹*First* of all, I'm going shopping on Saturday morning. ²_____ that I'm meeting some friends for lunch. What ³_____ you? What are you doing?

A: I don't ⁴_____ what I'm doing yet. What about you, Sam? ⁵_____ are your plans?

C: I'm going swimming in the morning. ⁶_____ I'm going to a football match.

3 Choose the correct responses.

1 What are you up to this evening?
  a And you?
  ⓑ Nothing much.
  c Great!

2 I'm going swimming on Saturday. What about you?
  a I don't have any plans yet.
  b Well done!
  c Yes, OK.

3 I'm going to a concert this weekend.
  a I don't know yet.
  b Nothing much.
  c That's nice.

4 First, I'm going to my tennis lesson.
  a I don't know yet.
  b Cool. Have you got any plans after that?
  c Come on!

4 Complete the dialogues with the phrases below.

| Don't be daft!   Seriously?   Wish me luck! |

1 A: What are you up to later this week?
  B: I've got exams on Thursday and Friday. _____

2 A: I'm running a marathon next weekend.
  B: _____ I didn't realise you were so fit!

3 A: Sailing isn't dangerous, is it?
  B: _____ It's perfectly safe!

5 🔊 17 Complete the dialogue with the words below. There are two extra words. Listen and check.

| about after ~~any~~ could daft doing first nothing plans probably seriously then |

Jen: Have you got ¹*any* plans for Saturday?

Leo: Yes, I've got quite a busy day. ²_____, I'm going to football training, as usual, and ³_____ that I'm going karting with my uncle. Have you ever done it? You drive these little mini racing cars round a race track.

Jen: That sounds cool!

Leo: Yeah. What ⁴_____ you? What are you ⁵_____ on Saturday?

Jen: ⁶_____ much. I'll ⁷_____ do my homework in the morning, but I don't know about the afternoon.

Leo: You ⁸_____ come karting with me if you want.

Jen: ⁹_____? That would be great! Won't your uncle mind?

Leo: Don't be ¹⁰_____! Of course he won't mind.

Jen: OK, cool! I can't wait!

I can write notes and make requests.

1 Complete the requests with the phrases below.

> could you please look   if it's OK with you
> let me know   would it be possible   ~~would you mind~~

1 *Would you mind* sending me Cara's address?
2 We could meet at my house. _____ if that's OK.
3 _____ to meet at seven o'clock?
4 _____, could we go on Saturday morning?
5 _____ in your car to see if my phone's there?

2 Match 1–5 with a–e to make sentences.

1 | b | Thanks for
2 | ☐ | Just a quick note
3 | ☐ | I had a
4 | ☐ | I really enjoyed
5 | ☐ | All the

a great time!
b ~~inviting me to go sailing with you.~~
c swimming in the sea.
d best, Jo.
e to thank you for taking me to the cinema.

3 Write the phrases below in the correct group.

> ~~Cheers!~~   Could you please send me the photos?
> Hi, there   Hey   I had a great time skiing.
> I loved snowboarding.   Let me know if that's OK.
> See you later.   Thanks for your message.

Greeting	Hi Hiya
Thanking the other person	Thanks for inviting me. Just a quick note to thank you for …
Introducing the topic	I really enjoyed taking part in the race.
Making a request	Would you mind keeping my jacket for me? Would it be possible to send me Tim's email address?
Ending	All the best. Bye! *Cheers!*

4 Complete the message with the phrases below.

> a great time   cheers   I loved   ~~just a quick~~
> would you mind

Hey,
[1]*Just a quick* note to thank you and your uncle for taking me karting last weekend. I had [2]_____ ! I've never done anything like that before and [3]_____ driving round the race track as fast as I could! I really enjoyed meeting your uncle too. He's cool!
I think I left my gloves in your uncle's car.
[4]_____ asking him if he could have a look for them?
[5]_____ !

Jen

5 Read the message. Write a note to Dave. Follow the instructions below.

I had a great weekend – Dave invited me to go kayaking with him and his uncle on the river. The water was really fast – that was exciting! And we had some races – great fun! Dave took some great photos – I must ask him to send them to me.

1 Use the message in Exercise 4 as a model.
2 Follow these steps:
   • Start your note in a suitable way.
   • Thank Dave for taking you kayaking.
   • Say what you enjoyed doing.
   • Ask Dave to send the photos to you.
   • End your note in a suitable way.

For each learning objective, tick (✓) the box that best matches your ability.

😊😊 = I understand and can help a friend.

😊 = I understand and can do it by myself.

🙁 = I understand but have some questions.

🙁🙁 = I do not understand.

		😊😊	😊	🙁	🙁🙁	Need help?	Now try ...
5.1	Vocabulary					Students' Book pp. 58–59 Workbook pp. 54–55	Ex. 1–2, p. 63
5.2	Grammar					Students' Book p. 60 Workbook p. 56	Ex. 3, p. 63
5.3	Reading					Students' Book p. 61 Workbook p. 57	
5.4	Grammar					Students' Book p. 62 Workbook p. 58	Ex. 4–5, p. 63
5.5	Listening					Students' Book p. 63 Workbook p. 59	
5.6	Speaking					Students' Book p. 64 Workbook p. 60	Ex. 6, p. 63
5.7	Writing					Students' Book p. 65 Workbook p. 61	

5.1   I can talk about sports and sports events.

5.2   I can talk about plans, predictions, arrangements and timetables.

5.3   I can identify specific detail in an article and talk about volunteering at a sports event.

5.4   I can talk about possible future situations.

5.5   I can identify specific detail in speech and talk about sports training.

5.6   I can ask and talk about plans.

5.7   I can write notes and make requests.

What can you remember from this unit?

New words I learned (the words you most want to remember from this unit)	**Expressions and phrases I liked** (any expressions or phrases you think sound nice, useful or funny)	**English I heard or read outside class** (e.g. from websites, books, adverts, films, music)

Vocabulary

1 Complete the sentences with the words below.

> basketball climbing diving ice-skating
> snowboarding yoga

1 Ali loves team sports. He plays for the school _____ team.
2 I don't like going underwater, so I hate _____!
3 I love winter sports – _____ is my favourite because I love coming down the mountain really fast!
4 In a _____ class, you move your body gently into different positions.
5 My sister's a good dancer, so she'd be good at _____ too.
6 You need very strong arms to do _____ because you have to lift your body up the side of a mountain.

2 Choose the correct option.

1 We couldn't play football because the *pitch / match* was too wet.
2 Manchester United wear a red and white *mascot / kit*.
3 The *fans / seats* all cheered when she scored.
4 The final *scoreboard / score* was 4–2.
5 I'd like to *do / play* yoga.
6 Do you *have / go* swimming lessons?
7 John is a really good football *play / player*.
8 You should *practise / practice* your skills every day.
9 I love water sports – I want to *take / set* up kayaking in the summer.

Grammar

3 Complete the sentences with the verbs below.

> 'll pay 'll win 'm going to take up 'm meeting
> opens 's going to score

1 The library _____ at nine o'clock tomorrow morning.
2 Don't worry – I'm sure you _____ the match tomorrow.
3 Look, Ronaldo's got the ball – he _____! Yes!
4 I _____ tennis next summer.
5 The film starts at eight. I _____ Tina at half past seven.
6 No, don't give me any money. I _____ for the tickets.

4 Complete the sentences with the correct form of the verbs in brackets.

1 I _____ fitter if I _____ running. (get, take up)
2 If you _____ regularly, you _____ into the team. (not practise, not get)
3 You _____ the race unless you _____ fast. (not win, run)
4 If it _____, we _____ table tennis indoors. (rain, play)
5 I _____ at four o'clock tomorrow unless my train _____ late. (arrive, be)

5 Decide if the sentences in each pair have the same meaning (S) or a different meaning (D).

1 ☐ a I won't call you unless there's a problem.
      b I'll only call you if there's a problem.
2 ☐ a We'll go swimming unless it's cold.
      b If it's cold, we'll go swimming.
3 ☐ a If Dan doesn't invite me to the party, I won't be upset.
      b I'll be upset unless Dan invites me to the party.
4 ☐ a I'll play in the match unless I'm ill.
      b I won't play in the match if I'm ill.

Speaking language practice

6 Complete the dialogues with the words and phrases below.

> don't know first got any plans nothing much
> then up to what about your plans

A

A: What are you [1] _____ at the weekend?
B: [2] _____. Just homework and watching TV, probably. [3] _____ you?
A: I [4] _____ yet. But Eddie wants to get together. Do you want to join us?
B: Yeah, cool!

B

A: Have you [5] _____ for Saturday?
B: Yeah. [6] _____, I'm going into town to buy some new trainers. [7] _____ I'm meeting Sam and we're going bowling. And you? What are [8] _____?
A: I don't have any plans yet. Maybe I'll come bowling with you.
B: Great!

1 Match 1–6 with a–f to make word friends.

1 [f] popular   a contact
2 [ ] huge   b posts
3 [ ] goal   c history
4 [ ] physical   d competition
5 [ ] national   e crowds
6 [ ] cultural   f ~~sport~~

2 Complete the sentences with the word friends in Exercise 1.

1 In my country the most *popular sport* is football.
2 However, it doesn't attract _____ anymore. Most people watch football on television.
3 I'm a goalkeeper. I stand between the _____.
4 The _____ of different football teams is fascinating, especially in countries like Spain or Brazil.
5 Football does not include as much _____ as rugby, but many players do get injured.
6 In my country the _____ for football is called the Premier League.

3 Match pictures A–E with verbs 1–5.

1 [E] throw   3 [ ] catch   5 [ ] hold
2 [ ] bounce   4 [ ] kick

A   B   C

D   E

4 Choose the correct option.

1 In basketball you have to (bounce) / *kick* the ball a lot.
2 You can't *kick* / *throw* the ball in handball.
3 You have to *kick* / *throw* the ball in football to score a goal.
4 You can't *hold* / *kick* the ball for a long time in most ball games.
5 The goalkeeper in football has to try to *catch* / *bounce* the ball and hold on to it.

5 Match 1–5 with a–e to make sentences.

1 [e] The Highland Games
2 [ ] The whole village
3 [ ] The Highland Games are now
4 [ ] People come every year here
5 [ ] The games are about

a to enjoy this traditional Scottish event.
b has gathered for this annual summer celebration.
c competing, of course, but they are also about community.
d celebrated more outside Scotland.
e ~~capture the cultural life and sports of this magical nation.~~

6 Complete the text with the words below.

> event ~~favourite~~ flat perfect straight
> symbol throw weighs

At most games the caber is people's
^{1}*favourite* sport. It is the final ^{2}_____
and a ^{3}_____ of the Highland Games.
The caber is about six metres long and
^{4}_____ around fifty-five kilograms.
Competitors have to ^{5}_____ it, then
flip it over and the caber has to land
^{6}_____. If it lands absolutely
^{7}_____, it's a ^{8}_____ throw.

7 Complete the sentences with the correct form of the verbs in brackets.

1 If you *like* (like) sports, you *will love* (love) the Highland Games!
2 You _____ (not know) what the Highland Games are like unless you _____ (take) part in them.
3 You _____ (see) the 'tossing the caber' competition if you _____ (stay) till the last day of the games.
4 If you _____ (not enjoy) sports or music, you _____ (not like) the Highland Games!
5 If you _____ (want) to try something different, try the Highland Games – you _____ (not regret) it!

8 Read the video script. Underline any words or phrases you don't know and find their meaning in your dictionary.

The Highland Games

Part 1

The Highland Games are a very old tradition. They were set up as way of bringing together Scotland's historical families. They capture the cultural life and sports of this magical nation.
5   They include the colours and symbols of a culture that almost disappeared, but is now stronger than ever. The Highland Games are a meeting place of strength, speed and celebration. Today on sports grounds, farmers' fields and city parks across this country, they are Scotland's very own Olympics!

10 This is the village of Ceres. It is home to Scotland's oldest Highland Games. For centuries the whole village has gathered for this annual summer celebration. For the people of Ceres, it's a day as important as Hogmanay – New Year's Eve in Scotland – or Christmas.

15 ### Part 2

The Highland Games are a mixture of fact and fantasy. They are a unique blend of sport and culture.

There is highland dancing, bagpipes and drums, and there is a series of sports too. There is usually athletics, sometimes cycling
20 and wrestling, but always the 'heavy events'. These include the stone shot, the hammer throw and tossing the caber.

At most games the caber is people's favourite sport. It's the final event and a symbol of the Highland Games. The caber is about six metres long and weighs around fifty-five kilograms. Competitors
25 have to throw it, then flip it over and the caber has to land flat. If it lands absolutely straight, it's a perfect throw.

The Highland Games are now also celebrated outside Scotland, in the USA, Canada, Australia and the Far East. These games are organised by families who emigrated from Scotland. The biggest
30 Highland Games in the world take place here, in the Blue Ridge Mountains in North Carolina. They last over four days and 22,000 people come every year to enjoy this traditional Scottish event of their ancestors.

The Highland Games are the most visible display of Scottish identity
35 that you can imagine. They are about competing, of course, but they are also about community, keeping tradition alive and making time for old friends. If you come, you won't regret it!

6

See the world!

6.1 | VOCABULARY | Travel

I can talk about holidays and travelling.

VOCABULARY
Types of holiday | At the hotel |
Equipment

GRAMMAR
Obligation, prohibition and advice |
Modal verbs for speculation

READING
True/False

LISTENING
Identifying specific details |
True/False

SPEAKING
Clarifying and asking for
clarification

ENGLISH IN USE
Time clauses

BBC CULTURE
Can ironing make
holidays exciting?

1 ● Order the words to make travelling phrases.

1 how / excuse / airport / do / get / me, / I / the / to / ?
Excuse me, how do I get to the airport?

2 train / I'd / to / buy / like / a / to / London / ticket
_____

3 me, / excuse / is / bus / a / near / there / here / station / ?
_____

4 time / the / train / what / leave / does / ?
_____

5 platform / what / arrive / train / does / at / the / ?
_____

2 ●● Complete responses a–e with the words below. Then match the responses with sentences 1–5 in Exercise 1.

| ~~end~~ platform p.m. return service |

a `3` Yes, it's at the *end* of the road.
b ☐ At 3.45 _____ .
c ☐ Single or _____ ?
d ☐ _____ 10.
e ☐ There's a bus _____ every twenty minutes.

3 ● Complete the words for types of holidays.

1 cr<u>u</u><u>i</u>se
2 a_t_v___y c___p
3 b___h h_l____y
4 c___y b___k
5 c___p__g t__p
6 s___ts____g h_l____y
7 b___p___i_g h_l___y

4 ●● Read the comments and write the type of holiday each person wants.

1 I'd love to visit some of the monuments in ancient Egypt.
sightseeing holiday

2 I'd like to go to Paris for a weekend. _____

3 My dream holiday would be to spend two weeks on a ship, visiting different places. _____

4 I want to just lie in the sun and swim in the sea! _____

5 I enjoy sleeping in a tent and cooking outdoors. _____

66

5 ● Match 1–5 with a–e to make sentences.

1 | b | We went to the reception first, | a | unless you make a reservation.
2 | ☐ | We're in a double | b | ~~to check in.~~
3 | ☐ | We met some of | c | pool and use all the hotel facilities.
4 | ☐ | We can swim in the | d | the other guests.
5 | ☐ | You won't get a room here | e | room on the third floor.

6 ●● Complete the review with the words below.

> check out   facilities   floor   guests   pool   ~~reception~~
> reservation   single   view

REVIEWS

★★★★

This is a great hotel and good value for money. The staff at the ¹*reception* desk were really friendly. I made my ² _____ online. I was travelling on my own, so I had a ³ _____ room. Ask for a room at the front of the hotel and on the top ⁴ _____ – they're a bit more expensive, but worth it for the ⁵ _____ of the beach. There's a ⁶ _____ where you can swim, but there are 300 ⁷ _____ in the hotel, so it's often quite busy. Other ⁸ _____ include a gym and a spa. Be careful: on the day you leave, you have to ⁹ _____ by ten o'clock. If you're late, they'll charge you for another day!

7 ● Look at the pictures and complete the words.

1 s**w i m s u i t**

2 r_ _ _ _ _ _ _

3 t_ _ _

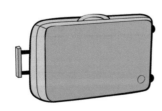

4 s_ _ _ _ _ _ _

5 g_ _ _ _ _ _ _

6 m_ _ _

8 ●● Write the correct word for each definition.

1 Men wear these to swim in. **t**runks
2 You use this to help you see at night. **t**_____
3 You put this on your skin so you don't burn in the sun. **s**_____ **c**_____
4 This is like a large bag that you can sleep in. **s**_____ **b**_____
5 You wear these to protect your eyes from the sun. **s**_____
6 You show this to officials when you enter a country. **p**_____

9 ●●● Complete the adverts with one word in each gap.

Global Holidays
This week's special offers

Seven days on the Mediterranean
A seven-day ¹*cruise* on a luxury ship. Travelling ² _____ sea is always relaxing and it's even better when the ship has fantastic ³ _____ like three cinemas and twelve different restaurants. Each morning explore ⁴ _____ foot, before setting sail for the next exciting destination.

£1,400 per person

A long weekend in New York
New York is a great place for a city ⁵ _____ . Enjoy the atmosphere of one of the world's great cities. The price includes a return ⁶ _____ to New York and a double ⁷ _____ in a city centre hotel.

£1,250 per person

A great value beach holiday
Spend six days lying on golden sands or swimming in clear blue seas on Kefalonia, a popular Greek island. Stay in a luxury hotel with a heated outdoor ⁸ _____ and an amazing restaurant serving real Greek food. All rooms have fantastic ⁹ _____ over the sea. If you fancy shopping, there's a regular bus ¹⁰ _____ into the nearest town.

£850 per person

I can talk about obligation, prohibition and advice.

1 ● **Match 1–5 with a–e to make sentences.**

1 [c] If you're tired, you
2 [ ] My sister's 18 now, so she
3 [ ] There's a bus service, so we
4 [ ] Your cousins live in Paris, so you
5 [ ] Weigh your suitcase – it

a mustn't weigh more than 15 kilos.
b ought to visit them while you're there.
c ~~should have a sleep.~~
d has to pay the full price for tickets.
e don't have to drive to the airport.

2 ●● **Complete the sentences with the verb forms below. There are three forms you don't need.**

> don't have to pay   must go   must spend
> mustn't pay   ~~mustn't worry~~   should drink
> shouldn't ask   shouldn't spend   will have to ask

1 You _mustn't worry_ about anything – everything will be fine!
2 We've already paid for the hotel, so we _____ for anything when we get there.
3 Madrid is a beautiful city – you really _____ there.
4 You _____ plenty of water when you're out in the sun all day.
5 I know I _____ so much money on holiday, but I just love shopping!
6 I'd love to go on a camping trip with you, but I _____ my parents first.

3 ●● **Complete the second sentence so it has the same meaning as the first. Use the word in capitals, and use between two and five words.**

1 I would advise you to look online for the best deals.
You _should look online_ for the best deals. (SHOULD)
2 It isn't necessary to buy tickets in advance.
You _____ tickets in advance. (HAVE)
3 You aren't allowed to take any liquids in your bag.
You _____ any liquids in your bag. (MUST)
4 It will be necessary to get a bus to the hotel.
We _____ a bus to the hotel. (HAVE)
5 It's a good idea to wear a sun hat when it's very hot.
You _____ a sun hat when it's very hot. (OUGHT)

4 ●●● **Complete the text. Choose the correct verb form for each gap.**

Top tips for backpackers

Travelling abroad is great fun, but there are a few simple rules you [1]_____ follow. First, you [2]_____ make sure you have all the documents you need – that's really important. You [3]_____ take a few simple first aid products like painkillers and plasters. And you [4]_____ forget your phone! Remember to keep in touch with your parents while you're away – you [5]_____ phone them every day, but you [6]_____ to phone or email at least once a week, otherwise they'll get worried. Look after your money and documents carefully while you're away. You [7]_____ keep your passport safe – you can face a lot of problems if you lose it. And remember the date and time of your flight home. If you miss your flight, you [8]_____ pay for another one, and it will probably be expensive!

1 a mustn't   c won't have to
  b don't have to   d have to
2 a shouldn't   c don't have to
  b must   d mustn't
3 a should   c don't have to
  b shouldn't   d ought
4 a must   c ought to
  b mustn't   d don't have to
5 a have to   c don't have to
  b must   d should
6 a mustn't   c don't have to
  b should   d ought
7 a ought   c must
  b mustn't   d don't have to
8 a should   c have to
  b don't have to   d will have to

5 Complete the dialogues with one word in each gap.

OUT of class

1 A: Remember to take some money with you so you can pay for the tickets.
  B: What do you _____ ? I thought they were free!
2 A: I'm sorry, I can't go to the cinema.
  B: In that _____ , I'll stay at home.

I can find specific detail in an article and talk about travelling.

1 WORD FRIENDS **Complete the sentences with the correct form of the verbs below.**

| explore go learn meet ~~plan~~ share |

1 We're *planning* a trip to Australia next year.
2 Shall we go and _____ the old part of the city?
3 I'd love to _____ Chinese, but I guess it's a very difficult language!
4 We usually _____ on holiday in August.
5 It's fun to make videos and _____ them with your friends online.
6 A backpacking holiday is a great way to _____ people.

2 **Read the article. Complete the sentences with one word in each gap.**

1 Gina decided to go to _____ as an exchange student.
2 She chose not to live in a _____ for her exchange year.
3 Most high schools in the USA have big _____.
4 Gina was surprised that the _____ was nice.
5 She enjoyed having _____ in the summer.
6 She was a _____ at her high school once.

3 **Read the text again. Mark the sentences T (true) or F (false).**

1 ☐ Gina didn't expect to have any problems with speaking English.
2 ☐ Mead is a small town in Colorado.
3 ☐ At first, Gina didn't find it easy being at an American school.
4 ☐ Not all the students at her high school were friendly.
5 ☐ Gina believes you can learn about other countries as a tourist as well as when you live there.
6 ☐ Her advice to other exchange students is to take part in lots of activities.

4 **Look at the words in italics in the sentences and find the word friends in the text. Then complete the sentences with the correct form of the verbs below.**

| admire consult experience go on have |

1 It's a good idea to _____ *a guidebook* before you visit a city.
2 If it's hot tomorrow, let's _____ *a barbecue*.
3 Every morning I wake up and _____ *the view* from my bedroom window.
4 What's the best way to _____ *the culture* of another country?
5 Would you like to _____ *an exchange* to another country?

An exchange student

We all love travelling to other countries, but how much do we really learn about the places we visit? We admire the view from our hotel room, we consult our guidebook and visit the popular tourist spots, then we return home with happy memories and 200 photos! But what's it like to live and study in another country?

Gina Rossi decided to spend a year in the USA as an exchange student. She knew the language would be difficult at first and she knew she would miss her friends back home, but she wanted to experience the real America.

Gina stayed with a family in Mead, Colorado. 'I didn't want to go to a city,' she says. Mead is a fairly small town, so it was ideal for her. What was the first thing that she noticed in America?

'Everything was bigger,' she says. 'The houses, the schools, the shops.' Gina found school life difficult at first. The classes in most high schools are very big and you have to be quite independent. And of course, everything was in English. But the teachers were excellent and the students were all really friendly. 'They soon made me feel at home,' she says. Did anything surprise her? 'I was expecting the food to be terrible,' she says. 'But the family I stayed with enjoyed cooking, so in fact, it was really nice. In the summer, when the weather was hot, we had a lot of barbecues – I liked those.'

Gina now says that living in a place, rather than visiting as a tourist, is the only way to experience the culture of another country. And her advice

for others? 'If you decide to go on an exchange, you should join in with everything, to make the most of the experience.' Gina even joined in as a cheerleader for a high school football game – but only once!

 **GRAMMAR** Modal verbs for speculation: *must, could, might/may, can't*

I can speculate about the present.

1 ● **Complete the sentences with *must* or *can't*.**

1 That tent's tiny! It *can't* be big enough for eight people!

2 Look, that _____ be our hotel over there – I recognise it from the website.

3 The boat trips are very popular, so they _____ be good!

4 Everyone's swimming in the sea, so the water _____ be too cold.

5 The food in that restaurant looks amazing, so it _____ be expensive!

6 That _____ be our bus – our bus isn't due until 10.30, and it's only ten o'clock.

2 ● **Choose the correct conclusion for each sentence.**

1 Tom's gone home early.
   ⓐ He might be ill.
   b He can't be ill.

2 I'm not sure where my phone is.
   a It must be in my bag.
   b It may be in my bag.

3 Carrie's shoes are black, but these ones are brown.
   a These could be Carrie's shoes.
   b These can't be Carrie's shoes.

4 I don't know where the museum is.
   a It might be near the station.
   b It can't be near the station.

5 Everyone's wearing T-shirts.
   a It must be hot.
   b It can't be hot.

6 I don't know what the museum's like. The guidebook doesn't mention it.
   a It might be interesting.   b It must be interesting.

3 ●● **Choose the correct answers.**

1 Look, that boy's standing up in the pool – it _____ be very deep.
   a may   ⓑ can't   c must

2 I guess this _____ be Jack's umbrella, but I'm not sure.
   a must   b can't   c could

3 There are hundreds of deckchairs on the beach. It _____ be a very popular beach!
   a must   b might   c can't

4 I'm not sure if the gym is open now – it _____ be closed.
   a can't   b may   c must

5 Camping _____ be fun in the rain – I guess everything gets horrible and wet!
   a must   b can't   c could

6 I don't know where he's from. I guess he _____ be French. Or maybe Spanish.
   a might   b must   c can't

4 ●●● **Complete the dialogue. Choose the correct option from the pairs of phrases below.**

> can't be expensive / must be expensive
> ~~can't be fun~~ / (might be fun)
> can't be lonely / could be lonely
> can't be right / may be right
> might be interested / must be interested
> must be scary / can't be scary

A: Have you seen this brochure for an activity camp?

B: Yeah, it looks good. It ¹*might be fun* to go on a holiday like this next summer. What do you think?

A: I agree. Do you think it costs a lot?

B: No, it ²_____ because it's for young people and they don't have much money.

A: That's true. What activities can you do?

B: Well, there's climbing. I don't know if I want to do that. I think it ³_____ being up so high.

A: Yes, you ⁴_____ about that, but the other activities look really good fun.

B: Yeah, I love canoeing. Do you think Abbie ⁵_____ in coming too? Should we ask her?

A: That's a good idea. I think it's definitely better to go with friends. It ⁶_____ if you go on your own and you don't know anyone.

I can identify specific detail in a conversation and talk about trips and excursions.

1 Choose the correct words to complete the sentences.

1 I think it's a good idea to _____ while you're still young.
   a trip   b journey   c travel

2 The hotel organises _____ to interesting tourist places.
   a excursions   b travels   c journeys

3 I enjoyed the day out, but the _____ back home took four hours!
   a travel   b journey   c excursion

4 We're planning a three-day _____ to New York next summer.
   a travel   b trip   c journey

5 Would you like to work in the _____ industry?
   a trip   b voyage   c travel

6 We were all tired after the long sea _____.
   a voyage   b travel   c journey

2 🔊 18 Listen to the first part of an interview. Which sentence is NOT true?

1 Ellie always goes on working holidays.
2 She has visited nine different countries.
3 She likes beach holidays.

3 🔊 19 Listen to the second part of the interview. Mark the sentences T (true) or F (false).

1 ☐ Ellie first found out about Woofing online.
2 ☐ Ellie always goes travelling when her job ends.
3 ☐ Ellie enjoys working at summer camps the most.
4 ☐ You can work at activity camps even if you aren't sporty.
5 ☐ You have to pay for food at activity camps.
6 ☐ Ellie thinks that working holidays might be difficult for older people.

4 🔊 19 Listen again. Write down the things below.

1 three sports that Ellie has taught _____, _____, _____
2 three disadvantages of working holidays _____, _____, _____
3 three advantages of working holidays _____, _____, _____

5 Match 1–6 with a–f to make compound nouns.

1 [c] a working   a trip
2 ☐ an organic   b desk
3 ☐ a weekend   c holiday
4 ☐ ski   d money
5 ☐ the reception   e farm
6 ☐ pocket   f season

6 Write the correct compound noun for each definition. Use the nouns in Exercise 5.

1 holiday where you do paid work
   working holiday
2 a small amount of money you receive each week _____
3 a farm that grows food without using chemicals _____
4 the part of a hotel where you check in when you arrive _____
5 a visit to a place on Saturday and Sunday _____
6 the period of time during the winter when there is enough snow to ski _____

I can clarify what I have said and ask for clarification.

1 Match 1–6 with a–f to make sentences.

1 [d] Can you speak
2 [ ] Sorry, I didn't
3 [ ] I was just
4 [ ] I just wanted to
5 [ ] Sorry, can you
6 [ ] What I said

a saying that Jo isn't usually late.
b was, that sounds a great idea.
c ask you about the Maths homework.
d ~~more slowly?~~
e catch that.
f say that again?

2 Order the sentences to make dialogues.

A
a [ ] What was that?
b [ ] I was just saying, there's a good film on at the cinema tonight.
c [1] Hey, Matt, there's a good film on at the cinema tonight.

B
a [ ] I said that Sam's busy so he can't come to the party.
b [ ] Maria can come to the party, but Sam's busy.
c [ ] Sorry, I didn't get the last part.

C
a [ ] I just wanted to ask you about Friday.
b [ ] Sorry, can you say that again?
c [ ] Hi, Lily. What time are we meeting on Friday?

3 Write the phrases below in the correct column.

| ~~Can you speak louder?~~ What was that? |
| Sorry, I didn't catch that. I said that ... |
| I was just saying ... What I asked was ... |
| Sorry, can you say that again? |
| Sorry, I didn't get the first part. |
| I just wanted to ask you about ... |

Asking for clarification	Clarifying
Can you speak louder?	

4 Complete the dialogues with sentences a–c.

OUT of class

1 A: Don't forget to pack your passport.
  B: Sorry, I didn't catch that. _____
  A: I said, don't forget to pack your passport.

2 A: Can you hear me better now?
  B: No, not really. I think it's my phone. _____ I can never get a good signal here. It drives me mad!

3 A: Can you bring your guidebook with you?
  B: Sorry, I didn't get the last part.
  A: I was just asking if you can bring your guidebook.
  B: What was that?
  A: _____ It's OK, I'll bring mine.

a Forget it.
b This is really annoying.
c You're breaking up.

5 🔊 20 Complete the dialogues with one word in each gap. Listen and check.

A
Jo: Hi, Tom. Are you going on the school trip in November?
Tom: Sorry, I didn't ¹*catch* that. The line's bad. You're ² _____ up a bit.
Jo: I just ³ _____ to ask you about the school trip in November.
Tom: Oh. Yeah, I'm definitely going!

B
Sam: We need to be at the airport at ten.
Jen: ⁴ _____ was that?
Sam: I ⁵ _____ that we need to be at the airport at ten.
Jen: OK.

C
Cara: Remember to pack your diving shoes because we might go diving if the sea's nice and clear.
Mike: Sorry, could you ⁶ _____ louder? I can't hear you.
Cara: ⁷ _____ I said was that you should pack your diving shoes. We might go diving.
Mike: Oh yeah. Good idea!

I can use time clauses.

1 Choose the correct option.

1 I'll keep an eye on your bag *after / (while)* you have a swim in the sea.

2 I'll call you *while / as soon as* I get back from my holiday.

3 *When / After* I see Paul, I'll ask him about his trip to China.

4 We'll tell someone where we're going *until / before* we go walking in the mountains.

5 Don't worry, we won't leave for the airport *until / after* you get here.

6 We can go away *after / while* I finish all my exams.

7 I'll let you know *when / while* I find my passport.

8 Let's wait *after / until* the queue is a bit shorter and then go through security.

2 Complete the sentences with the correct form of the verbs below.

> arrive   be   find   leave   ~~open~~   take off

1 We'll wait here until the ticket office *opens* .

2 They'll serve food after the plane _____.

3 I'll email you when we _____ in New York.

4 I'll feel homesick as soon as I _____ home!

5 We'll have something to eat when we _____ a nice restaurant.

6 I'll look after Rex while you _____ away.

3 Find and correct the mistakes in the sentences.

1 We'll go as soon as the weather will improve.
We'll go as soon as the weather improves.

2 The boat won't leave until everyone will be on board.

_____

3 As soon as the sun will come out, I'll take some photos.

_____

4 When we'll get to the hotel, we'll feel much happier.

_____

4 Add a comma if necessary.

1 When we arrive, I'll call you.

2 We'll check the weather before we set out.

3 While we're waiting we'll have a sandwich.

4 We'll stay here until it stops raining.

5 I'll send you the link when I get home.

5 Complete the second sentence so that it means the same as the first sentence. Use no more than three words.

1 We'll only eat when everyone gets here.
We *won't eat* until everyone gets here.

2 I'll go to Peru and then to Egypt.
I'll go to Egypt _____ to Peru.

3 When it stops raining, we'll leave immediately.
We'll leave as soon _____ raining.

4 I'll check my passport and then pack my clothes.
I'll check my passport _____ I pack my clothes.

5 He'll only be happy when he gets his money back.
He won't be happy _____ his money back.

6 Read the advert. Choose the correct answers.

A summer job at sea!

We need young people to work on our ships this summer. You'll work as part of our childcare service so that busy parents can relax ¹_____ their children happy.

²_____ on board one of our ships, you'll feel what a magical place it is to work! There are so many exciting things to see and do!

³_____ work each day, you'll be able to enjoy the amazing facilities on board – swimming pools, a gym, and eight fantastic restaurants.

If you want to have fun this summer ⁴_____ money, fill in the application form <u>here</u>.

1   a while you'll keep   c until you keep
    ⓑ while you keep   d before you keep

2   a When you'll come   c As soon as you come
    b Until you come   d When you came

3   a After you finish   b When you'll finish
    c While you finish   d Until you finish

4   a when you'll earn   b before you earn
    c while you earn   d after you'll earn

For each learning objective, tick (✓) the box that best matches your ability.

☺☺ = I understand and can help a friend. ☹ = I understand but have some questions.

☺ = I understand and can do it by myself. ☹☹ = I do not understand.

		☺☺	☺	☹	☹☹	Need help?	Now try ...
6.1	Vocabulary					Students' Book pp. 70–71 Workbook pp. 66–67	Ex. 1–2, p. 75
6.2	Grammar					Students' Book p. 72 Workbook p. 68	Ex. 3, p. 75
6.3	Reading					Students' Book p. 73 Workbook p. 69	
6.4	Grammar					Students' Book p. 74 Workbook p. 70	Ex. 4, p. 75
6.5	Listening					Students' Book p. 75 Workbook p. 71	
6.6	Speaking					Students' Book p. 76 Workbook p. 72	Ex. 6, p. 75
6.7	English in Use					Students' Book p. 77 Workbook p. 73	Ex. 5, p. 75

6.1   I can talk about holidays and travelling.
6.2   I can talk about obligation, prohibition and advice.
6.3   I can find specific detail in an article and talk about travelling.
6.4   I can speculate about the present.
6.5   I can identify specific detail in a conversation and talk about trips and excursions.
6.6   I can clarify what I have said and ask for clarification.
6.7   I can use time clauses.

What can you remember from this unit?

New words I learned (the words you most want to remember from this unit)	**Expressions and phrases I liked** (any expressions or phrases you think sound nice, useful or funny)	**English I heard or read outside class** (e.g. from websites, books, adverts, films, music)

Vocabulary

1 Complete the sentences with the words below. There are two extra words.

> backpacking break camp
> cruise platform return
> ticket trip

1 What _____ does the train leave from?
2 I'd like a train _____ to London, please.
3 We're planning a camping _____ this summer.
4 We went on a three-week _____ and really loved being on the ship.
5 She's just been on a city _____ to Paris for the weekend.
6 You can do lots of different sports at the activity _____.

2 Choose the correct option.

1 You can make a *reservation / reception* online.
2 Wow! There's a beautiful *pool / view* from this window!
3 There are two of us, so we need a *single / double* room, please.
4 I wear *sunglasses / sun cream* to protect my eyes from the bright sun.
5 A *tent / torch* will help you see in the dark.
6 You can find details about the museum in the *guidebook / trunks*.
7 It's a three-day *journey / travel* to reach this village in the mountains.
8 I'd love to *trip / travel* around India.

Grammar

3 Match sentences 1–6 with conclusions a–i. There are three extra conclusions.

1 ☐ I'm not sure whose coat this is.
2 ☐ It's only eight o'clock, but Tania's gone to bed!
3 ☐ I don't know when Max gets back from holiday.
4 ☐ You've just had a very big lunch.
5 ☐ I don't know where my passport is.
6 ☐ No one's in the sea today.

a It can't be very cold.
b It could be tomorrow.
c You can't be hungry!
d It must be next week.
e It may be in my bedroom.
f It might be John's.
g She can't be ill.
h It must be too cold.
i She must be tired.

4 Choose the correct answers.

1 I'm going to go to bed _____ home.
  a as soon as I get b while I get
2 I'll ask Maria about her holiday _____ her.
  a until I see b when I see
3 We need to get everything tidy _____ home!
  a before Mum gets b before Mum will get
4 I'll finish packing _____ a taxi.
  a while you'll call b while you call
5 The cafe's closed, but we'll wait here _____.
  a when it will open b until it opens
6 I'll call you _____ my homework.
  a after I finish b when I'll finish

Speaking language practice

5 Complete the dialogues with the phrases below.

> didn't catch first part I said that
> just saying say that again what I asked

1 A: Have you printed your plane ticket?
  B: Sorry, I _____ that.
  A: _____ was if you've printed your plane ticket.
2 A: Sara's picking us up at eight and Tom's meeting us at the airport.
  B: Sorry, I didn't get the _____.
  A: _____ Sara's picking us up at eight.
3 A: There's a special offer on cruises at the moment.
  B: Sorry, can you _____?
  A: Yes, I was _____ there's a special offer on cruises at the moment. Are you interested?

1 Match the words below with the photos.

> adventure holiday   sightseeing
> ~~sunbathing~~   voluntourism

1   *sunbathing*

2   _____

3   _____

4   _____

2 Match word friends 1–6 with definitions a–f.

1   `d`   budget airlines
2   ☐   preferred option
3   ☐   key factor
4   ☐   ex-pat communities
5   ☐   friendly reputation
6   ☐   great attraction

a   an important element
b   a group of foreign residents
c   a general opinion that people are nice
d   ~~low-cost travel by plane~~
e   a place lots of people visit
f   the choice you like the best

3 Complete the advert with the words below.

> activity   camping   landscapes   preferred option
> ~~sightseeing~~   sunbathing   trekking

Tired of the usual holidays of ¹*sightseeing* and
²_____ on the beach? Come ³_____
with us in the Pyrenees! You'll see beautiful
⁴_____ and feel at one with nature!
We don't offer ⁵_____ – our guests'
⁶_____ is to stay in shelters with a
real bed for the night.

**Sign up today for an ⁷_____ holiday
you'll never forget!**

4 Choose the correct option according to
the video.

1   The sea *location* /(*temperature*) in the
    Maldives is wonderful.
2   You can do lots of sports there, like *scuba* /
    ski diving.
3   The ride to the glacier in Iceland can be
    long and *rough* / *snowy*.
4   The *fast* / *top* speed in a snowmobile is
    ninety-five kilometres per hour.
5   The lovely thing about the hot-air balloon
    experience is the total *silence* / *perspective*.

5 Complete the sentences about the video with
the modal verbs below.

> can't   could   don't have to   ~~have to~~   might
> must   shouldn't

1   You *have to* take plenty of money on these
    holidays.
2   You _____ travel alone when
    snowmobiling – it's not a very good idea.
3   You _____ do the hot-air ballooning more
    cheaply with other people.
4   You _____ annoy people doing jet skiing,
    so don't do it for long!
5   It _____ be that difficult to do
    snowmobiling – I bet it's really easy.
6   It _____ be beautiful to be up in a balloon
    looking at those views.
7   You _____ go to Iceland to do
    snowmobiling – there are lots of cold places!

6 Complete the blog post with the correct form
of the verbs below.

> ~~blow~~   break   fall   melt   shine

Today was the first time I tried
snowmobiling in Iceland. I really loved it!
The weather was weird. The wind
¹*was blowing* really hard, but it didn't
matter too much because the sun
²_____ all day. In fact, it is quite
warm for February, so the ice
³_____ a lot. But I was careful driving over the glacier.
It was beautiful at the beginning of day. The dawn
⁴_____ at about seven o'clock. As the days are so short
here in the winter, I could see the night ⁵_____ as well.
A really memorable day!

7 Read the video script. Underline any words or phrases you don't know and find their meaning in your dictionary.

Adventures of a lifetime

Part 1

These are the Maldives, a beautiful series of islands located in the Indian Ocean, where the sun is always shining. It's popular with travellers looking for a luxury option. In fact, most tourists here have their own private island for total relaxation! But further out to sea,
5 there are more energetic options.

Meet our hosts, Kirstie and Phil. Here in the Indian Ocean the sea temperature is a wonderful twenty-seven degrees Celsius – just perfect for swimming, snorkeling, scuba diving, fishing, windsurfing and the sport we're going to see now: jet skiing! Kirstie is nervous at first, but she soon gets the idea.
10 This is the most popular and comfortable model because you can sit down in it. You can go up to 80 kilometres per hour, so it's better to hold on tight! Jet skiing is great fun, but expensive. Other tourists might also get annoyed by the noise, so it's best to do it for short lengths of time.

Part 2

15 Kirstie and Phil are now off to a much colder place. In fact, the temperature has dropped to minus twenty degrees Celsius. They have come to Iceland to try their next adventure sport: snowmobiling!

Here glaciers cover eleven percent of the country, but they are not easy to get to. Kirstie and Phil have to travel in a specially prepared 4x4 vehicle. It's a long and a bit of a rough
20 ride! The landscape looks like the surface of the moon. In fact, astronauts came here to practise for their expeditions.

Obviously, to ride one of these vehicles, you need to wear special protective clothing. The good news is that the accelerator and handle bars are heated! The snowmobile's top speed is ninety-five kilometres per hour, but the terrain here is tough, so Kirstie and Phil are
25 taking it easy.

With snowmobiling, you should always follow your guide's advice. It's best to do it when snow has just fallen. If not, you might fall through the snow when the ice melts. It can be very dangerous. Again, it's not a cheap option, but the landscapes are unique, especially as night falls over the glacier.

30 ## Part 3

Kirstie and Phil's final adventure holiday is a much more relaxing option: hot-air ballooning! They are now in Morocco, between the city of Marrakech and the Atlas Mountains. There's only one drawback: to do this sport, you have to get up really early. Balloons fly in the early morning before the wind starts to blow. It's six o'clock in the
35 morning now. The sun is rising over the Atlas, the sky is blue, but the stars are still out. It's a beautiful moment as the dawn breaks.

Compared to the other sports we've seen, the wonderful thing about flying in a hot-air balloon is the slowness and the total silence. You feel like you're floating and the views are stunning. You see everything from such a different perspective. Yes, it's the perfect place
40 to get away from it all, but it's also the most expensive of all the trips. If you want to do it more cheaply, you can share a balloon with other travellers. Enjoy the ride!

7

Getting to know you

VOCABULARY
Family and friends | Phrasal verbs

GRAMMAR
Second Conditional | Defining and non-defining relative clauses

READING
True / False

LISTENING
Identifying specific details | Multiple choice

SPEAKING
Identifying people

WRITING
A short story

BBC CULTURE
Is moving house good for you?

7.1 **VOCABULARY** Family and friends

I can talk about relationships with family and friends.

1 ● Choose the correct answers.

1 Who shares one parent with you, but not two parents?
   a your stepson   (b) your half-brother

2 Who is your mother's mother?
   a your great-grandmother   b your grandmother

3 If your mother marries again, who is the man?
   a your grandfather   b your stepfather

4 Who is your father's grandfather?
   a your great-grandfather   b your great-great-grandfather

5 If your father marries again and his new wife already has two daughters, who are they?
   a your half-sisters   b your stepsisters

2 ●● Read the comments and write the family words.

1 Tom's the same age as me and I really like him. His mum's married to my dad now, but I'm only related to him by marriage, not by blood. He's my *stepbrother* .

2 Elsie is my dad's mother, so she's my _____. She's nearly seventy, but she still does a lot of sport!

3 Lucy's the youngest in my family and she's my _____. We have the same mum, but we have different dads.

4 My mum died when I was quite young. My dad's got a new wife now, called Sara. I really like her, and I call her Mum, even though she isn't my real mother. She's my _____.

5 The oldest person in my family is Albert. He's eighty-nine and he's my mum's grandfather, so he's my _____.

3 ● Choose the correct option.

1 I *go* / (*get*) on really well with my cousin Jack – he's great!

2 You should talk to someone if you have a problem – don't just deal *for* / *with* it on your own.

3 I really enjoy *hanging* / *holding* out with my friends.

4 If you're feeling lonely, you should go *out* / *over* and meet some new people.

5 I *got* / *fell* out with Tania last week, but we soon sorted things out and we're friends again now.

6 I share a bedroom with my sister, but I can't *put* / *get* up with all her mess. I want my own room!

78

4 ●● Complete the sentences with the correct form of the phrasal verbs below.

> deal with   fall out with   ~~get on with~~   go out   hang out with   put up with

1 I don't *get on with* my sister at all – we're completely different and she just annoys me!
2 It's very difficult to _____ problems such as bullying on your own. It's much easier if you ask a teacher for help.
3 When I moved to a new school, I _____ a lot because I wanted to make new friends.
4 I can't _____ noise when I'm trying to study. I need silence.
5 I prefer to _____ just a small group of friends. I don't like big crowds.
6 I _____ Dale because he kept asking me to do his homework for him and it really annoyed me!

5 ● **WORD FRIENDS** Look at the pictures. Choose the correct sentences.

1 (a) She likes spending time on her own.
   b She always sees her friends after school.

2 a They don't share any interests.
   b They have the same sense of humour.

3 a They're having an argument.
   b They're getting to know each other.

6 ●● Complete the sentences with the words below. There are two extra words.

> backgrounds   ~~get~~   enjoy
> have   nerves   own   see
> sense   share   spend

1 I'm quite a shy person – it takes me a while to *get* to know people.
2 I love being with other people and I hate spending time on my _____ .
3 Flossie and I get on well and we _____ each other's company.
4 Jo and Beth come from similar _____ , so they have a lot in common.
5 It really gets on my _____ when my sister borrows my clothes without asking!
6 My friends and I usually _____ each other at the weekend.
7 I think it's important for friends to have the same _____ of humour.
8 My brothers and I _____ a lot of time together, especially in the school holidays.

7 ●●● Complete the text with one word in each gap.

Your problems – Emma's here to help!

My mum and dad got divorced two years ago and my dad has just remarried. I really don't ¹*get* on with his wife, my new ² _____ . She's also got two daughters already, so I've now got two ³ _____ . I know I should be happy for my dad, but this woman really gets ⁴ _____ my nerves and I don't ⁵ _____ any interests with her kids! I just stay in my bedroom all the time now because I don't know how to ⁶ _____ with this situation. Help!

Emma says: *It can be difficult when a parent remarries, especially when there are also new children to add to your family. It will take time for you to ⁷ _____ to know your dad's new wife, so just be patient. But hopefully, if you make the effort and ⁸ _____ some time with her daughters, you will find that things improve.*

Have your say! 2 comments

Amelia24 This happened to me two years ago when my mum remarried. I ⁹ _____ a lot of arguments with my new dad and I even ended up shouting at my mum and ¹⁰ _____ out with her, which was awful. You have to give the new relationships time.

SaraG Don't spend too much time at home if you find it stressful. ¹¹ _____ out when you can and hang ¹² _____ with your friends at weekends, rather than spending time ¹³ _____ your own at home. The others are right – it takes time, but I'm sure that if you make the effort with your new family members, in time you will all enjoy ¹⁴ _____ other's company.

I can talk about imaginary situations.

1 ● Match 1–6 with a–f to make sentences.

1 [d] Sam would do better in exams
2 [ ] If I didn't have any friends,
3 [ ] You wouldn't be so tired
4 [ ] If you had the chance to go travelling,
5 [ ] Would you be pleased
6 [ ] If I were you,

a I'd be really lonely.
b if your friends organised a party for you?
c I'd talk to someone about your problems.
d ~~if he worked harder.~~
e if you went to bed earlier.
f which countries would you visit?

2 ● Choose the correct option.

1 I *will be* / (*would be*) really happy if my dad *would get* / (*got*) married again.
2 What *would* / *will* you do if your best friend *was* / *would be* upset with you?
3 If I *had* / *would have* plenty of money, I *will take* / *would take* all my friends out for a meal.
4 Lottie *will be* / *would be* more popular if she *wasn't* / *wouldn't be* so moody!
5 If I *were* / *would be* you, I *don't worry* / *wouldn't worry* about what other people think of you.
6 If Max *wouldn't talk* / *didn't talk* so much in class, his teachers *don't get* / *wouldn't get* so angry with him.

3 ●● Complete the second sentence so that it means the same as the first sentence. Use the Second Conditional.

1 I have a lot of exams this year, so I'm really stressed.
I *wouldn't be* so stressed if I *didn't have* a lot of exams this year.
2 Carrie is unfit because she doesn't do any exercise.
If Carrie _____ some exercise, she _____ fitter.
3 Jack's parents always get worried because he never tells them where he's going.
Jack's parents _____ worried if he _____ them where he was going.
4 I'm not old enough to watch that film.
I _____ that film if I _____ older.
5 I don't have a big house, so I won't invite many people to the party.
I _____ more people to the party if I _____ a bigger house.
6 You shouldn't spend all your money on clothes.
If I _____ you, I _____ all your money on clothes.

4 ●● Complete the text messages with the correct form of the verbs below. Use the Second Conditional.

| be (x2) buy ~~have~~ know like |
| not remember not worry |

Hi, Jenna! Help! I need some advice. It's Abi's birthday next Saturday and I don't know what to give her. If I ¹*had* plenty of money, I ² _____ her something nice to wear because I know she ³ _____ that. But I've only got a few pounds. What can I do?

If I ⁴ _____ you, I ⁵ _____ about buying expensive gifts. That's not what friendship is about. Sure, Abi ⁶ _____ upset if you ⁷ _____ her birthday, but I'm sure she'd feel bad if she ⁸ _____ you were so worried. Just relax! Buy her some flowers and give her a big birthday hug!

5 ●●● Complete the article with one word in each gap.

Money or friends?

What ¹*would* you do if you won £10 million? ² _____ you had that amount of money, you ³ _____ need to work – ever! Just imagine that! If you ⁴ _____ have to work, you ⁵ _____ be able to spend your life travelling or relaxing – doing exactly what you wanted. Does that sound good to you?

Most people imagine that if they ⁶ _____ rich, they would ⁷ _____ happier. They think that if money ⁸ _____ not a problem for them, they ⁹ _____ have any worries in the world. But in reality, it seems this isn't true. Psychologists have found that what really makes us happy is our family and friends, and money can't buy those. So, if you ¹⁰ _____ choose between money and friends, which ¹¹ _____ you go for?

I can find specific detail in an article and talk about friends.

1 Complete the words in the sentences.

1 Your m_a_t_e_s are your friends.

2 Your c_ _ _ _ m_ _ _ _ _s are the friends you have in your class at school.

3 Your b_ _ _t friends are the ones you like the most.

4 Someone who doesn't like you and tries to hurt you is your e_ _ _ _y.

5 Jodie h_ _ _ a lot of friends.

6 Marie wants to b_ friends with me.

2 Read the article. Mark the sentences T (true) or F (false).

1 ☐ You pay a rent-a-friend website to choose a friend for you.

2 ☐ The first rent-a-friend websites were in the United States.

3 ☐ People in Japan are often too busy to spend time with friends.

4 ☐ Lia hasn't made many new friends in London.

5 ☐ Lia thinks you could make real friends by using a rent-a-friend website.

6 ☐ Tom thinks it takes time to make real friends, but it is worth waiting in order to have genuine friends.

3 Find word friends with *friend* and *friendship* in the text. Then complete the sentences with the words below.

| circle   close   form   ~~make~~

1 Some people don't find it easy to *make* new friends.

2 Everyone needs _____ friends that they can talk to when they have problems.

3 Sam's a very popular guy – he has a big _____ of friends!

4 It can take time to _____ a real friendship with someone.

4 Find phrases 1–4 in the text. Then match them with definitions a–d.

1 [c] get in touch with   a do exercise in a gym

2 ☐ work out   b find by chance

3 ☐ catch on   c ~~contact~~

4 ☐ come across   d become popular

Would you rent a friend?

We all know it can be difficult to make new friends when you move to a new place, but would you ever consider paying someone to be your friend? This is the service that a rent-a-friend website offers. The idea is simple: you look through the online profiles and select someone you think you would get on with, then you get in touch with them. For a small fee, the person will meet you and spend time with you, doing whatever you want to do – working out at the gym, watching a movie or just playing computer games.

The biggest rent-a-friend websites are in the USA, where the idea has really caught on, especially in big cities such as New York. But the idea originated in Japan, where many people's lives

are so full of working or studying that they have little time for socialising and forming genuine friendships. There are also now websites available in the UK and several other countries.

We asked our readers what they thought and some of you were in favour of the idea. Lia, from North London, thought it could be a good way to meet new people. She moved to London when she was sixteen and had to leave all her close friends behind in Manchester. 'It was quite hard at first,' she says, 'and I was a bit lonely for a while.' She now has a big circle of friends, but she says that if she moved again, she would consider the idea of renting a friend. 'Sometimes when you're new to a place, you just want to

get out and do something, but it isn't much fun going to the cinema on your own. I think it would be fun to meet someone in this way – you might even come across your new best friend!'

Tom, who lives in Scotland, doesn't agree. He believes that friends are a really important part of our life and we shouldn't devalue the idea of friendship by making it into something that you can buy and sell instantly. 'If I moved to a new city,' he says, 'I'd put the effort into getting to know my new classmates and form friendships with them. It might take a bit longer, but it's better than buying fake friends.'

Have your say! Comment below.

I can be specific about people, things and places.

1 ● **Complete the sentences with clauses a–f.**

1 The house _e_ has got a big garden.

2 The men _____ both had dark hair.

3 The car _____ is quite old.

4 There's a small café on the beach, _____ .

5 My new bike, _____ , is amazing!

6 Mrs Perks, _____ , is a dance teacher.

a where they sell really nice ice creams

b which my mum drives

c who lives in my street

d that I saw near the bank

e ~~that my parents want to buy~~

f which I ride every day

2 ●● **Read the article. Choose the correct answers.**

Real friends?

Do you think of all the people ¹_____ you know online as your friends? It seems that a lot of the people ²_____ use social media sites such as Facebook have over 200 online friends, compared to around fifty 'real' friends, ³_____ they actually meet in real life. Facebook, ⁴_____ was started in 2004, now has over 1.5 billion users worldwide, and a lot of people see it as a place ⁵_____ they can meet new friends as well as keeping in touch with old ones. Studies ⁶_____ have looked at how people behave on social media sites have found that people are sometimes more honest and open online than they are in real life. But psychologists say, it is our ten or twelve closest relationships ⁷_____ are the most important to us. So maybe it's still better to meet your friends in the local park or café, ⁸_____ you can talk face to face.

1 a which   ⓑ who   c where   d what

2 a that   b where   c what   d which

3 a which   b that   c who   d where

4 a what   b which   c who   d that

5 a which   b that   c who   d where

6 a that   b who   c where   d what

7 a who   b where   c which   d what

8 a which   b who   c that   d where

3 ●● **Combine the sentences using relative clauses. Use *who*, *which* or *where*. Add commas where necessary.**

1 My cousin is very good at football. He's three years older than me.
My cousin, *who is three years older than me, is* very good at football.

2 Edinburgh is about 600 kilometres from London. It's the capital of Scotland.
Edinburgh _____ about 600 kilometres from London.

3 Jo showed me the house. She lived there when she was younger.
Jo showed me _____ when she was younger.

4 We met a man. He grows vegetables for the market.
We met a man _____ for the market.

5 Bournemouth is on the coast. My grandparents live there.
Bournemouth _____ on the coast.

6 The film was very good. We saw it last week.
The film _____ very good.

4 ●●● **Find and correct the mistakes in the sentences. Remember to check for commas. Two sentences are correct.**

1 That's the café which we sometimes have lunch.
That's the café where we sometimes have lunch.

2 The prize that we won wasn't very exciting.

3 Sophie who is French can speak French and English.

4 We don't know all the people that live in our street.

5 Their car, that is over ten years old, still works well.

6 I lent the book to Dan, which loves adventure stories.

I can identify specific information in a monologue and understand different meanings of get.

1 **WORD FRIENDS** What does *get* mean in each sentence? Choose the correct option.

1 We didn't get home until after midnight!
   become /(arrive)/ leave

2 I get bored quite quickly if I have nothing to do.
   make / bring / become

3 I got an email from my uncle yesterday.
   received / arrived / wrote

4 I need to get some new jeans.
   make / change / buy

5 My brother is trying to get a job.
   pay / find / leave

6 Shall I get you a drink?
   take / drink / bring

2 🔊 **21** Listen to a teacher talking about a buddy system for students with autism in her school. Choose the correct answers.

1 What does the teacher say about autism?
   a It's a disability.
   b It isn't very common.
   c It can cause social problems for some students.

2 When are buddies most needed?
   a during lessons
   b at break time
   c before and after school

3 What is the best description of a buddy?
   a a helper
   b a best friend
   c a teacher

4 What has surprised the teachers?
   a The buddies have learned a lot from the experience.
   b There are now fewer students with autism.
   c Students with autism now have fewer problems in class.

3 🔊 **22** Listen to Joey talking about being a buddy. Choose the correct answers.

1 What do we learn about Joey and Matt?
   a They were friends before the buddy scheme started.
   b They are in the same class.
   c They share the same friends.

2 What did Matt find difficult at break times?
   a chatting to people
   b spending time alone
   c joining in with activities

3 What did Joey help Matt to do?
   a become better at sport
   b have the confidence to make friends
   c cope with people who are strange

4 What has Joey learned from the experience?
   a Everyone can play football.
   b It isn't easy to make friends.
   c It's OK to be different.

4 🔊 **23** Complete the sentences with the phrases below. Listen and check.

> get into   get involved   gets quite stressed
> got a lot out of   ~~got back~~

1 I first started being a buddy to Matt when I *got back* to school after the summer holidays.

2 He explained that he _____ if he's surrounded by people the whole time.

3 If there's a big activity going on, he finds it difficult to _____ .

4 If he gets a bit better, I think he'll _____ the school team!

5 I've _____ the whole experience of being a buddy.

I can explain who I am talking about.

1 Complete the words in the definitions of people at a wedding.

1 The b r *i* d e is the woman who is getting married.

2 The b _____ g _____ m is the man who is getting married.

3 A b _____ m _____ d is a good friend who helps the woman who is getting married.

4 A p _____ b _____ y is a young boy who helps the woman who is getting married.

5 The g _____ s are the people who come to watch the wedding.

2 Match 1–6 with a–f to make questions.

1 [*f*] Who's the boy on
2 [ ] Who's the girl who is
3 [ ] Who's that guy next
4 [ ] Which one
5 [ ] Who's the woman at
6 [ ] Who's the young child in

a wearing a blue dress?
b do you mean?
c the front, by the door?
d the middle?
e to your grandmother?
f ~~the left?~~

3 Complete the sentences with the words below.

back   near   one   playing   standing
~~talking~~   tall   wearing

1 That's Paul, there. He's *talking* to my Uncle George.

2 Look, there's my Aunt Paula. She's at the _____, behind my cousin Freddie.

3 She's _____ a really nice dress.

4 Toby's on the left, _____ the bridegroom.

5 There's my cousin Dave. He's _____ next to my brother Matty, looking a bit bored!

6 That's my little cousin Tilly. She's _____ with a ball. Look, she's really cute!

7 Mike's the _____ who is wearing a red tie.

8 Abigail's the _____ one, in the pink dress.

4 Complete the dialogues with the phrases below.

OUT of class

| Boo!   It'll be a laugh.   Pass it here. |
| ~~What are you up to?~~ |

1 A: Hi, Jen. *What are you up to?*
   B: I'm just showing Tara my holiday photos. Do you want to see them?

2 A: _____
   B: Oh Brett! You scared me! How are you?

3 A: What's that?
   B: It's my brother's graduation photo.
   A: Oh, let's see it. _____
   B: OK. There you are.

4 A: Do you want to see the photos from my end-of-year party?
   B: Yeah, why not? _____ It's always funny looking at other people's photos.

5 🔊 24 Complete the dialogue with the words below. There are two extra words. Listen and check.

| at   bride   cute   let's   on   pageboy |
| sitting   ~~up~~   wearing   which |

Liz: Hi, there. What are you two [1] *up* to?

Kim: I'm just showing Mark the photos from my family party last month. Remember? It was my granddad's seventieth birthday. Look, that's me and my cousin Beth.

Liz: [2] _____ see. Oh yeah. She looks nice.

Kim: She is. We get on really well.

Mark: Who's that little boy?

Kim: [3] _____ one?

Mark: The one [4] _____ the left, behind you. The one who's [5] _____ a blue jumper.

Kim: Oh that's my half-brother. He was a [6] _____ at my sister's wedding last year.

Liz: Aw! He's [7] _____! And who's that guy who's [8] _____ next to your brother?

Kim: That's my cousin Jack. He lives in Manchester.

Liz: Hmm, he's quite good-looking! Can I meet him some time?

I can write a short story.

1 Read the story. Choose the correct answers.

1 What does Emma tell us to set the scene?
a She wants to make some new friends.
b She wants to celebrate the end of exams.

2 What is the first event in the story?
a Emma talks to Cara.
b Emma invites Alfie and George.

3 What is the second event in the story?
a Emma decides that the new girl is boring.
b Emma decides to invite the new girl.

4 What is the climax of the story?
a Bethanie gets on well with everyone.
b Cara is bored at the party.

Making a new friend

Last weekend I wanted to celebrate the end of exams.
I decided to invite a few friends round to my house
to watch a movie and have some pizza. First, I asked
Cara. She's my best friend. 'Cool! Great idea,' she
said, so I was really pleased.

Next, we planned who else to invite. 'You should
invite Alfie and George,' Cara said. 'They're always
good fun.' I agreed and I added them to my list.

Just then, I noticed the new girl in our class. She was
very quiet and she didn't really speak to anyone. To
be honest, I thought she was a bit boring. 'I think
I'll invite the new girl,' I said. I went over to her and
asked her. 'I'd love to,' she said.

That weekend we had a great time. Everyone got
on well with each other and the new girl, Bethanie,
wasn't boring at all. In fact, she made us all laugh a
lot and we're now good friends! In future I won't be
so quick to judge people before I get to know them.

2 Write the underlined phrases and sentences from the story in the correct group.

Starting your story and setting the scene	Last week it was my birthday. *Last weekend I wanted to celebrate the end of exams.*
Introducing your characters	Cara's in the same class as me. _____
Using time words and phrases to show the order of events	First, _____ _____
Using direct speech	'You should invite Alfie and George,' Cara said. _____ _____
Ending your story	I learned an important lesson that day.

3 Complete the sentences with the time words below.

| afterwards   just   ~~last~~   that |

1 *Last* week it was my birthday.
2 _____ then, I noticed a girl who was standing on her own.
3 _____ day I made a new friend.
4 _____ , she invited me round to her house.

4 Rewrite the direct speech with the correct punctuation.

1 I'm having a party next weekend I said
'I'm having a party next weekend,' I said.

2 Would you like to come to my party I asked
_____

3 I'd love to come to the party he said but I can't
_____

4 I think that's a great idea she said
_____

5 Write a story about organising an event and making a new friend. Follow the instructions below.

1 Use the story in Exercise 1 as a model.
2 Follow these steps and say:
• what event you wanted to organise.
• what you did or who you spoke to first.
• what you talked about and planned next.
• who else you decided to invite and why.
• what happened at the event.
• what you learnt from the experience.

For each learning objective, tick (✓) the box that best matches your ability.

☺☺ = I understand and can help a friend.   ☹ = I understand but have some questions.

☺ = I understand and can do it by myself.   ☹☹ = I do not understand.

		☺☺	☺	☹	☹☹	Need help?	Now try ...
7.1	Vocabulary					Students' Book pp. 82–83 Workbook pp. 78–79	Ex. 1–2, p. 87
7.2	Grammar					Students' Book p. 84 Workbook p. 80	Ex. 3, p. 87
7.3	Reading					Students' Book p. 85 Workbook p. 81	
7.4	Grammar					Students' Book p. 86 Workbook p. 82	Ex. 4–5, p. 87
7.5	Listening					Students' Book p. 87 Workbook p. 83	
7.6	Speaking					Students' Book p. 88 Workbook p. 84	Ex. 6, p. 87
7.7	Writing					Students' Book p. 89 Workbook p. 85	

7.1   I can talk about relationships with family and friends.
7.2   I can talk about imaginary situations.
7.3   I can find specific detail in an article and talk about friends.
7.4   I can be specific about people, things and places.
7.5   I can identify specific information in a monologue and understand different meanings of *get*.
7.6   I can explain who I am talking about.
7.7   I can write a short story.

What can you remember from this unit?

New words I learned (the words you most want to remember from this unit)	**Expressions and phrases I liked** (any expressions or phrases you think sound nice, useful or funny)	**English I heard or read outside class** (e.g. from websites, books, adverts, films, music)

Vocabulary

1 Match words 1–6 with definitions a–f.

1 ☐ grandfather   4 ☐ stepbrother
2 ☐ great-grandmother   5 ☐ stepmother
3 ☐ half-sister   6 ☐ stepson

a a woman who is married to your father, who is not your real mother

b the father of your mother or father

c a girl who shares one parent with you, but not both parents

d a boy who is the child of the woman a man is married to, but not his child

e the son of your stepfather or stepmother, who is related to you by marriage, not by blood

f the mother of your grandmother

2 Choose the correct option.

1 Who do you usually *hold / hang* out with after school?

2 Don't get angry – I don't want to fall *out / off* with you!

3 His teachers said they wouldn't *put / keep* up with his bad behaviour any longer.

4 Dan and I have the same *feeling / sense* of humour.

5 We are always *doing / having* arguments.

6 Sara and I have a lot *in / for* common.

7 Peggy *went / got* a bit upset when I told her about the accident.

8 Kitty *has / keeps* loads of friends!

Grammar

3 Complete the Second Conditional sentences with the correct form of the verbs in brackets.

1 If you _____ more time studying, you _____ better exam results! (spend, get)

2 We _____ to the beach every day if it _____ sunny. (go, be)

3 If I _____ lots of money, I _____ all over the world. (have, travel)

4 I _____ to someone about this problem if I _____ you. (talk, be)

5 She _____ more exercise if she _____ near a gym. (do, live)

6 If I _____ drawing, I _____ Art at university. (enjoy, study)

4 Choose the correct option.

1 The boy *who / which / where* sits next to me in class is called Max.

2 That's the park *that / which / where* we sometimes hang out after school.

3 There's a new boy in my class, *which / that / who* comes from Spain.

4 Their house, *that / who / which* is in the town centre, is quite big.

5 Is that the bike *who / that / where* you got for your birthday?

6 There's a boating lake in the park, *which / where / that* you can hire boats.

5 Rewrite the sentences adding the information in brackets as a non-defining relative clause. Add commas where necessary.

1 My grandmother is still very active. (is seventy-six)
My _____ active.

2 My uncle works at the main hospital in the city. (is a doctor)
My _____ in the city.

3 Bournemouth is on the south coast. (my cousins live)
Bournemouth _____ south coast.

4 His new bike is really light. (he got for his birthday)
His new _____ light.

5 Andy suggested going to the pizza restaurant in town. (they do really nice pizzas)
Andy _____ really nice pizzas.

Speaking language practice

6 Complete the dialogues with the phrases below.

> a laugh   at the back   do you mean
> she's wearing   tall one   up to   who's that boy

A

A: Hi, Lizzy. What are you [1]_____ ?

B: I'm just showing Katie the photos from my sister's wedding. Do you want to see them?

A: Sure. It'll be [2]_____ .

B

A: [3]_____ on the left?

B: Which one [4]_____ ?

A: The [5]_____ with dark hair, on the right.

C

A: That's my Auntie Lucy there, [6]_____ .

B: Oh yes. [7]_____ a really nice dress!

1 Match 1–6 with a–f to make word friends.

1 | d | community   **a** problem
2 | ☐ | sense of   **b** family
3 | ☐ | image   **c** people
4 | ☐ | retired   **d** ~~spirit~~
5 | ☐ | big happy   **e** identity
6 | ☐ | rootless   **f** couples

2 Complete the sentences with the word friends in Exercise 1.

1 There are many _rootless people_ in the world today. They are always moving from one place to another.

2 Many _____ live in mobile homes in beach areas. It can be a very relaxing way to live when you have stopped working.

3 Some trailer parks have an _____, but they are not as bad as they seem.

4 He helped a lot of people in society and demonstrated a great _____.

5 Being part of a club can give people a _____.

6 Everybody was very friendly – they were like a _____ for me.

3 Choose the correct option.

1 Everybody in the trailer park (gets on with)/ goes out with each other. They are all friends.

2 If you have to *put up with / deal with* a serious problem, sometimes it's good to ask for help.

3 If you don't know what to do tonight, you can *fall out with / hang out with* us.

4 You should *go ahead / go forward* and try mobile living sometime. You have nothing to lose!

5 You shouldn't *stare at / laugh at* people who are homeless. It's not funny at all.

4 Complete the sentences with the correct form of the verbs in brackets.

1 If the Dolgan people didn't move house regularly, the reindeer _would die_ (die).

2 What would you do if you _____ (live) in the Arctic?

3 I _____ (not feel) bad if I lived in the Arctic. I like the cold!

4 If I could choose, I _____ (live) nearer my family.

5 I would move to another country if I _____ (have) more money.

5 Complete the sentences with the adjectives below.

> essential   extended   nomadic   perfect
> raw   ~~typical~~   valuable

1 We are far above the Arctic Circle and this is a _typical_ Dolgan village.

2 Good relationships are _____ here, so they all get on well.

3 Reindeer are so _____ that people only eat them if they have to.

4 Their favourite food is _____ fish from the frozen rivers.

5 This Dolgan village is home to just two _____ families.

6 Over a year, these _____ people travel hundreds of miles across the vast frozen tundra.

7 Here, man and reindeer live in _____ harmony.

6 Choose the correct option. Which relative pronouns can be replaced with *that*?

1 Survival is only possible because of reindeer fur, (which)/ who makes very warm clothing.

2 This is the village *which / where* the Dolgan people live.

3 The children, *who / which* are still very young, help with all the work they can.

4 The Arctic, *where / which* hardly anybody lives, is one of the hardest places on earth to survive.

5 We enjoyed the video about the Dolgans *who / which* the teacher showed in class.

7 Read the video script. Underline any words or phrases you don't know and find their meaning in your dictionary.

On the move

It is winter. We are far above the Arctic Circle and this is a typical Dolgan village. It is home to just two extended families. These people, who are originally from central Asia, came here during the eighteenth
5 century to look after reindeer. Here, in the coldest part of the Arctic, life is very hard. The only way to get water for nine months of the year is to melt ice from the frozen rivers.

Outside it is absolutely freezing, with temperatures in
10 the winter as low as -40°C. Survival is only possible because of reindeer fur, which makes very warm clothing. This warm clothing is especially important for the children. But the Dolgan even use reindeer fur to insulate their huts as well.

15 Community is very important to the Dolgan people. Everybody helps each other. Good relationships are essential here, so they all get on well. Reindeer are so valuable that the people only eat them if they have to. Their favourite food is raw fish from the frozen rivers.

20 Every week or so, these families get ready to travel once more. They must find new grounds for their herds. If they didn't move, the reindeer would die because of the lack of food. First, they round up their strongest animals with lassos. This is a skill which their
25 ancestors brought with them from central Asia. Then, literally, they move house. There is a lot to carry, but a whole Dolgan village can be taken down and moved in just a few hours. Over a year, these nomadic people travel hundreds of miles like this across the vast frozen
30 tundra.

The first Dolgan people came to the Arctic a long time ago because of the large number of reindeer all over this area. Their ancestors still follow the same lifestyle today. Here man and reindeer live in perfect
35 harmony. Moving is not just good for them – they could not live in any other way.

8

No time for crime

VOCABULARY
Criminals | The law | Action verbs

GRAMMAR
Present and Past Simple passive |
have/get something done

READING
Multiple choice

LISTENING
Identifying main points |
Multiple choice

SPEAKING
Persuading and reassuring

ENGLISH IN USE
Negative prefixes for
adjectives

BBC CULTURE
Is chewing gum a crime?

I can talk about crime and criminals.

1 ● Complete the words in the definitions.

1 A t*h i*ef takes things that belong to other people.
2 A v_____l breaks things in public places.
3 A p____p_____t takes small things from your pocket.
4 A s____l____r takes things from shops without paying.
5 A b_____r goes into people's homes and takes things.
6 A r_____r takes money from a bank or business.

2 ● **WORD FRIENDS** Look at pictures A–D and complete
sentences 1–5 with the words below.

| ~~breaking into~~ committing damaging robbing stealing |

A   B   C   D

1 The man in picture A is *breaking into* someone's house.
2 The woman in picture B is _____ some jewellery.
3 The men in picture C are _____ a bank.
4 The man in picture D is _____ a car.
5 The people in the pictures are all _____ crimes.

3 ● **WORD BUILDING** Choose the correct option.

1 The police finally caught the (burglars) / burglaries.
2 We're lucky because there isn't much *vandals / vandalism*
   in this town.
3 The bank *robbers / robberies* got away with over £500,000.
4 They accused her of *shoplifters / shoplifting*, but she said she
   was only trying the coat on.
5 A *pickpocket / pickpocketing* stole my phone.
6 She is very upset by the *thief / theft* of her jewels.

4 ● Match 1–6 with a–f to make sentences.

1 [c] She had to pay a £300
2 [ ] The bank has offered a
3 [ ] I want to study
4 [ ] The judge didn't send
   him to
5 [ ] What would be a
   suitable
6 [ ] You will need a good

a reward of £10,000 for
   information about the
   crime.
b punishment for this crime?
c ~~fine for shoplifting.~~
d lawyer to persuade the
   judge you are innocent.
e prison because he was
   so young.
f Law at university.

5 ●● Complete the sentences with the words below. There is one extra word.

> court ~~jail~~ judge law lawyer punishment reward

1 Matt spent fifteen years in *jail* for his crimes.
2 Everyone in the _____ was shocked by the details of this terrible crime.
3 He can expect to receive a harsh _____ for this crime.
4 The _____ listens to the evidence and decides how long someone should spend in prison.
5 If you break the _____, you will be punished.
6 Jen got a _____ of £50 for taking the missing bag to the police station.

6 ●● Choose the correct answers.

1 The police _____ the thieves down the street.
   a escaped (b) chased c fell
2 Be careful you don't _____ off that wall!
   a fall   b push   c pull
3 Don't leave your shoes there. Someone will _____ over them.
   a climb   b chase   c trip
4 There were over twenty police officers there, but the robbers still managed to _____!
   a escape   b chase   c trip
5 She hurt her back because someone _____ her down the stairs.
   a fell   b pushed   c jumped
6 He managed to _____ out of the window and get away.
   a climb   b pull   c chase

7 ●●● Read the texts. Choose the correct answers.

The Westbury Times

They need to learn a lesson!
Two teenagers were arrested for ¹_____ their school building yesterday. The two boys broke windows in the building and sprayed paint over it. The police said the community would not put up with ²_____ of this kind. The teenagers are too young to go to ³_____, but the police hope the ⁴_____ they receive will be serious enough to teach them a lesson.

Information needed
The police are asking for help from the public after ⁵_____ got away with two valuable paintings. The criminals ⁶_____ into the town's art gallery and ⁷_____ the two paintings last night. The alarm sounded at the gallery and the police arrived, but the criminals managed to ⁸_____ through a back door. The art gallery is offering a ⁹_____ of £10,000 for the safe return of the two paintings.

Brave grandmother catches a criminal
Seventy-two-year-old grandmother Beryl Bridges was shocked when she saw a ¹⁰_____ stealing someone's wallet near the station on Saturday. She ¹¹_____ after the man and caught him when he ¹²_____ and fell. 'It makes me really angry when people ¹³_____ crimes,' Beryl said. 'They shouldn't get away with it!' The man will appear in ¹⁴_____ tomorrow.

1	a robbing	(b) damaging	c stealing	d committing
2	a burglar	b burglary	c vandal	d vandalism
3	a jail	b fine	c reward	d judge
4	a law	b punishment	c court	d reward
5	a shoplifters	b vandals	c thieves	d pickpockets
6	a put	b broke	c sent	d escaped
7	a robbed	b committed	c stole	d put
8	a escape	b chase	c pull	d catch
9	a fine	b reward	c punishment	d law
10	a shoplifter	b vandal	c pickpocket	d burglar
11	a fell	b pulled	c pushed	d chased
12	a escaped	b tripped	c pulled	d pushed
13	a commit	b do	c have	d get
14	a judge	b law	c fine	d court

I can use verbs in the Passive.

1 ● **Complete the table. Which four verbs are regular?**

Verb	Past Simple	Past Participle
ask	asked	[1]asked
catch	[2]_____	caught
chase	chased	[3]_____
hide	[4]_____	hidden
know	knew	[5]_____
make	[6]_____	made
read	read	[7]_____
see	[8]_____	seen
sell	sold	[9]_____
use	[10]_____	used
watch	watched	[11]_____
write	[12]_____	written

2 ● **Choose the correct option.**

1 The two robbers *was* / *were* caught as they were leaving the bank.

2 A lot of science *is* / *are* used to solve crimes nowadays.

3 A secret microphone *was* / *were* hidden under her clothes.

4 Sometimes ordinary people *is* / *are* asked to help the police with information.

5 CCTV cameras *isn't* / *aren't* used in the shopping centre.

6 The thieves *wasn't* / *weren't* seen by anyone.

3 ● **Order the words to make sentences.**

1 my / stolen / purse / pickpocket / was / a / by
   My purse was stolen by a pickpocket.

2 every year / a lot of / mobile phones / stolen / are
   _____

3 asked / she / a lot of questions / the police / by / was
   _____

4 some / reported / aren't / to / the police / crimes
   _____

5 your / car / when / stolen / was / ?
   _____

6 CCTV cameras / are / here / used / ?
   _____

4 ●● **Complete the second sentence so that it means the same as the first sentence. Use no more than three words.**

1 They hid the paintings in the back of their van.
   The paintings *were hidden in* the back of their van.

2 People don't use guns in many robberies.
   Guns _____ in many robberies.

3 A shop assistant caught the shoplifter.
   The shoplifter _____ a shop assistant.

4 Millions of people watch crime dramas on TV.
   Crime dramas _____ millions of people on TV.

5 Did they send the thief to prison?
   Was _____ to prison?

6 People steal a lot of jewellery from this shop.
   A lot of jewellery _____ this shop.

7 They didn't find the missing money.
   The missing money _____ .

8 Do they send children to prison there?
   _____ to prison there?

5 ●●● **Complete the article with the correct passive form of the verbs below.**

announce ~~create~~ help know make publish solve watch

The Belgian detective

The character of the Belgian detective Hercule Poirot [1]**was created** by the writer Agatha Christie in the 1920s. Between 1920 and 1975 over 800 Poirot novels and short stories [2]_____ . In the stories, Poirot sometimes works alone, but usually he [3]_____ by his assistant, Captain Hastings. Poirot always dresses smartly and he [4]_____ for his neat moustache and his polite manners. He is very intelligent and believes that all crimes [5]_____ by using the 'little grey cells' in your brain.

A lot of the Poirot stories [6]_____ into popular films in the 1970s, and even today stories about Poirot [7]_____ by millions of people each year on TV. When, finally, Poirot's death [8]_____ in a 1975 novel, an article about his life appeared in the newspaper *The Times*, as if he had been a real person!

I can find specific detail in an article and talk about solving crimes.

1 **Complete the words in the sentences.**

1 The police are interviewing a w i t n e s s who saw the robbery take place.

2 It will take a very clever d_ _ _ _ _t_ _e to catch this criminal!

3 The police questioned the s_ _p_ _t, but he didn't admit that he was guilty.

4 This is a very difficult c_ _e because there is very little evidence.

5 The police found Morton's f_ _ _ _ _ _ _p_ _ _ _s on the murder weapon.

6 The thieves were seen on the C_ _V c_ _ _ _ _s in the shop.

2 **Read the article. Choose the correct answers.**

1 What does the writer say about the first CSI shows?
 a They attracted a lot of criticism.
 b They were less popular than *CSI New York*.
 c They were popular immediately.
 d Everything about them was new.

2 What do we learn about the work of CSIs in the series?
 a They work closely with the police.
 b Their jobs seem to be very exciting.
 c They develop new scientific techniques to solve crimes.
 d They usually solve crimes through science alone.

3 How is real life different, according to the writer?
 a In real life the police only use old-fashioned ways of solving crimes.
 b CSIs never leave their laboratories in real life.
 c The job of a real CSI is very boring.
 d CSIs in real life don't catch criminals.

4 What effect has the TV series had?
 a It has encouraged more young people to study science.
 b It has reduced the amount of crime.
 c It has encouraged more people to join the police.
 d Criminals learned to avoid leaving evidence at crime scenes.

5 What is the writer's main aim in the text?
 a to describe the TV series in detail
 b to explain how real CSIs catch criminals
 c to discuss how realistic the series is
 d to encourage people to learn more about the work of CSIs

CSI: fact or fiction?

When the American crime series *CSI (Crime Scene Investigation)* was first shown on TV in 2000, it was an immediate hit and soon led on to more shows such as *CSI New York* and *CSI Miami*. The series took the traditional idea of a detective story, but showed for the first time how modern scientific methods are used to study things such as fingerprints, hair and blood samples in order to solve crimes. Despite some criticisms, the series has continued to be very popular and is watched by millions of people around the world.

In the series, the investigators are shown as having quite glamorous lives. They are usually the first people to arrive at the scene of a crime. Working as a team, they eventually manage to catch the bad guys using both high-tech science and traditional police detective work. The real police seem to be irrelevant, as the Crime Scene Investigators interview witnesses, question suspects and often catch the criminals after dramatic chase scenes.

Of course, this isn't quite the same as the real world. In real life it's the police who question suspects and solve crimes. Although science can help the police, old-fashioned ways of investigating crimes are still very important. It's true that real CSIs visit crime scenes, but the majority of their work after that takes place in the laboratory. They are scientists, trying to make sense of the samples they have collected. This doesn't mean their work is boring, but it isn't as exciting as in the TV series and they certainly don't get involved in arresting criminals.

The *CSI* series has had a big impact. It has made people aware of all the detailed work that is needed to help the police solve crimes. Some people were worried that the series might teach criminals how to

avoid being caught, but this hasn't happened. There is still a lot of crime, and criminals are still leaving plenty of clues. The popularity of the series has led to an increased interest in science subjects among young people who are keen to become tomorrow's CSIs. Let's hope they aren't disappointed by the reality of the job!

I can use the construction *have/get something done*.

1 ● Order the words to make sentences.

1 last summer / had / I / painted / my / bedroom
I had my bedroom painted last summer.

2 get / teeth / you / your / should / regularly / checked
_____

3 sofa / can / you / delivered / have / the / to your house
_____

4 often / how / cleaned / the / you / do / get / windows / ?
_____

5 stolen / his / wallet / last week / he / had
_____

6 getting / dress / a / she's / for her wedding / made
_____

2 ●● Look at the pictures and complete the sentences with the correct form of the verbs below.

get/clean ~~get/cut~~ get/repair have/steal
have/take have/test

1 She *gets* her hair *cut* once a month.

2 He needs to _____ his car _____.

3 He's _____ his eyes _____ right now.

4 They all love _____ their photo _____.

5 She _____ her bike _____ yesterday.

6 He needs to _____ his watch _____.

3 ●● Complete the second sentence so that it means the same as the first sentence, using the verbs in brackets. Use no more than four words.

1 We could ask someone to deliver a pizza if you like. (get)
We could *get a pizza delivered* if you like.

2 I want someone to pierce my ears. (have)
I want to _____.

3 An expert designed their garden. (had)
They _____ by an expert.

4 You should ask a doctor to check that injury. (get)
You should _____ by a doctor.

4 ●●● Complete the text with the correct form of the verbs below.

get/check   get/fit   get/put up
have/connect   ~~have/make~~   have/replace

Can you burglar-proof your house?

Maybe not completely, but security experts think it is worth [1]*having* a few changes *made* to your home to make it safer. A lot of people think [2]_____ a sign _____ saying 'Beware of the dog' is a good idea, but according to the experts, most criminals know that family pets aren't usually dangerous. Locks are important, though. You should [3]_____ any old locks _____ with more modern ones. Modern locks are harder for criminals to open. It's also a good idea to [4]_____ an alarm _____. You can [5]_____ the alarm _____ to the local police station so the police are alerted immediately. If you're uncertain about what changes to make to your home, you should think about [6]_____ your home _____ by a security expert.

5 Complete the dialogues with one word in each gap.

OUT of class

1 A: What's in this pan?
B: Watch _____. It's hot!

2 A: Tess is going to organise the food for the party.
B: That's _____. Now we need to decide who to invite.

LISTENING and VOCABULARY — A crime

I can identify main points in speech and talk about discovering a crime.

1 **WORD FRIENDS** Complete the text with the words below.

area   clues   crime   criminal   fingerprints   witnesses

> When you get to a crime scene, it's important to search the
> ¹_area_ first and look for ²_____ . Then you should interview
> all the ³_____ and take ⁴_____ of any suspects. When
> you are sure who is guilty, you can arrest the ⁵_____ and
> solve the ⁶_____ !

2 **25** Listen to some people talking about crimes. Choose the correct answers.

1 What did the thieves take?

A

B

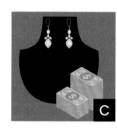
C

2 What was Dan doing when the burglary happened?

A

B

C

3 What did the vandals do?

A

B

C

4 What happened at the station?

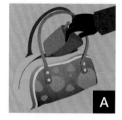
A

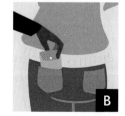
B

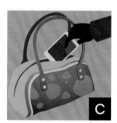
C

5 Who stole the computer game?

A

B

C

3 **26** Listen to a police officer talking about a crime. Order the events.

a ☐ Sergeant Linfield went to the house.

b ☐ Police officers took fingerprints and looked for clues.

c ☐ Sergeant Linfield called the number labelled 'Home'.

d ☐ Mrs Jones found a mobile phone in the garden.

e ☐1 Mr and Mrs Jones reported a burglary.

f ☐ Sergeant Linfield caught the burglar.

g ☐ Sergeant Linfield interviewed Mr and Mrs Jones.

4 **27** Listen to a news report. Complete the notes.

> Place of robbery:
> ¹_____ on Park Street
>
> Date of robbery:
> ²_____
>
> Amount of money stolen:
> ³ £_____
>
> Number of suspects:
> ⁴_____
>
> Colour of suspects' car:
> ⁵_____
>
> Number to call if you have information:
> ⁶_____

I can persuade and reassure someone.

1 Complete the sentences with the words below.

| ~~come~~ course fine practise try worry |

1 *Come* on! It's not difficult!
2 I know you haven't done it before. Just _____ it. You might like it!
3 Of _____ you can do it!
4 Don't _____! Everything will be OK.
5 You'll be _____!
6 I know you're not very good at it yet. Just _____ a bit more and try again.

2 Match 1–6 with a–f to make sentences.

1 [e] I don't   a I can do it.
2 [ ] It's   b try.
3 [ ] I'm sure you   c you try?
4 [ ] I suppose   d alright.
5 [ ] OK, I'll   e ~~know.~~
6 [ ] Why don't   f can do it.

3 Write the phrases below in the correct column.

| ~~Come on!~~ Don't worry! I don't know.
I know you can do it. I suppose I can do it.
It's OK. Just try it. OK, I'll try. Please! |

Persuading someone	Reassuring someone	Responding
Come on!		

4 Choose the correct responses.

1 I feel really nervous!
  a Please!
  (b) You'll be fine.
  c I don't know.
2 I don't know if I'll enjoy acting.
  a OK, I'll try.
  b I don't know.
  c Why don't you try?
3 Of course you can do it!
  a OK, I'll try.
  b Come on!
  c Please!
4 What if I make a mistake?
  a I suppose I can do it.
  b Don't worry!
  c Please!

5 Complete the dialogues with the phrases below.

| Can you give me a hand?
Off you go.   Oh my goodness! |

1 A: Hi, Charlie!
  B: _____ You gave me a fright. I didn't know you were there.
  A: Sorry!
2 A: This box is really heavy.
  B: _____
  B: Of course.
3 A: I have to go now, to catch my bus.
  B: OK. _____ I'll see you later.

6 🔊 28 Complete the dialogues with the words below. There are two extra words. Listen and check.

| course fine just know please suppose
sure try ~~worry~~ |

A
Amy: Hi, Sam. You don't look very happy.
Sam: No, I'm not. I've got my English speaking exam in about half an hour.
Amy: Don't [1]*worry*! It'll be [2]_____. You're really good at English.
Sam: I don't [3]_____. Sometimes I just forget everything in exams.
Amy: I'm [4]_____ you can do it! Good luck!
Sam: Thanks, Amy.

B
Sara: Hi, Jade. Rob and I are going ice-skating on Saturday. Do you want to come?
Jade: I don't know. I've never done ice-skating before.
Sara: Oh [5]_____! It'll be fun.
Jade: But what if I can't do it?
Sara: Of [6]_____ you can do it! You're really good at sport.
Jade: OK, I'll [7]_____.
Sara: Great!

I can form and use negative adjectives.

1 Write the negative form of the adjectives below in the correct group.

~~comfortable~~ correct healthy honest
legal logical patient pleased possible
regular relevant visible

Negative prefix	Negative adjective
un-	*uncomfortable*, _____
dis-	_____, _____
im-	_____, _____
in-	_____, _____
il-	_____, _____
ir-	_____, _____

2 Match the negative form of the adjectives below with the definitions.

correct ~~intelligent~~ interesting legible
polite usual

1 *unintelligent*: not clever
2 _____: not normal
3 _____: very difficult to read
4 _____: not right
5 _____: rude
6 _____: boring

3 Complete the sentences with negative adjectives from Exercises 1 and 2.

1 Henry hates waiting. He's really *impatient*.
2 I can't read your handwriting. It's so messy it's completely _____!
3 Chocolate is very bad for you. It's really _____.
4 No one can walk on water – it's _____!
5 If you do something _____, the police will come after you.
6 That's a very _____ plant – I've never seen one like it before.

4 Choose the correct option.

1 I don't like sitting on this chair. It's *irregular /* (*uncomfortable*).
2 These creatures are so small that you can't see them. They're *invisible / irresponsible*.
3 Jack never tells the truth. He's *illegible / dishonest*.
4 I didn't do my homework, so my teacher was *unusual / displeased*.
5 This isn't a real clue. It's very *irrelevant / impossible*.
6 I didn't enjoy that lesson. It was really *displeased / uninteresting*.

5 Read the article. Choose the correct answers.

THE ART OF POLICE WORK

Everyone would agree that being a police officer is a very [1]_____ job, and it is important to catch people who behave in [2]_____ ways. But it isn't always easy to find the person who has committed a crime, and sometimes the police make mistakes. Sometimes officers are [3]_____ to find the criminal who has committed a terrible crime and sometimes they act too quickly because they are worried the public will be [4]_____ if they don't catch someone quickly. Individual officers can sometimes act in [5]_____ ways too, and believe someone is guilty just because they don't like them. The way to do good police work is always to follow all the clues in a [6]_____ way, even if they seem small and [7]_____. The results that this leads to may sometimes be [8]_____, but hopefully, they will be [9]_____.

1 (a) responsible   c legible
  b irresponsible   d illegible
2 a honest   c regular
  b dishonest   d irregular
3 a usual   c patient
  b unusual   d impatient
4 a logical   c pleased
  b illogical   d displeased
5 a fair   c important
  b unfair   d unimportant
6 a possible   c logical
  b impossible   d illogical
7 a important   c pleased
  b unimportant   d displeased
8 a intelligent   c expected
  b unintelligent   d unexpected
9 a correct   c patient
  b incorrect   d impatient

8.8 SELF-ASSESSMENT

For each learning objective, tick (✓) the box that best matches your ability.

☺☺ = I understand and can help a friend.   ☹ = I understand but have some questions.

☺ = I understand and can do it by myself.   ☹☹ = I do not understand.

		☺☺	☺	☹	☹☹	Need help?	Now try ...
8.1	Vocabulary					Students' Book pp. 94–95 Workbook pp. 90–91	Ex. 1–3, p. 99
8.2	Grammar					Students' Book p. 96 Workbook p. 92	Ex. 4, p. 99
8.3	Reading					Students' Book p. 97 Workbook p. 93	
8.4	Grammar					Students' Book p. 98 Workbook p. 94	Ex. 5, p. 99
8.5	Listening					Students' Book p. 99 Workbook p. 95	
8.6	Speaking					Students' Book p. 100 Workbook p. 96	Ex. 7, p. 99
8.7	English in Use					Students' Book p. 101 Workbook p. 97	Ex. 6, p. 99

8.1   I can talk about crime and criminals.
8.2   I can use verbs in the Passive.
8.3   I can find specific detail in an article and talk about solving crimes.
8.4   I can use the construction *have/get something done.*
8.5   I can identify main points in speech and talk about discovering a crime.
8.6   I can persuade and reassure someone.
8.7   I can form and use negative adjectives.

What can you remember from this unit?

New words I learned (the words you most want to remember from this unit)	**Expressions and phrases I liked** (any expressions or phrases you think sound nice, useful or funny)	**English I heard or read outside class** (e.g. from websites, books, adverts, films, music)

Vocabulary

1 Match the words below with the definitions.

> fine   jail   judge   shoplifter   theft   vandal

1 someone who steals things from shops
  _____

2 an amount of money that someone has to pay as a punishment _____

3 a place where criminals are sent as a punishment _____

4 someone who damages buildings or things in public places _____

5 the crime of stealing things
  _____

6 someone in a court who decides what punishment a criminal should receive
  _____

2 Choose the correct option.

1 They *climbed / pulled* out of the window when the fire got out of control.

2 The two men were accused of *stealing / robbing* a bank.

3 We must find out who *committed / made* this crime.

4 She *chased / tripped* the pickpocket down the street.

5 Someone *sent / broke* into our house last night.

6 Hurry up – we need to *fall / escape*!

3 Complete the sentences with the words below. There are two extra words.

> arrest   clue   detective   fingerprints   look
> solve   suspect   witness

1 I'm sure we can _____ this crime.

2 The police took his _____ and found they were the same as the ones on the gun.

3 It is the job of the police to _____ criminals.

4 There was only one _____ who saw what happened.

5 The police thought that the watch was an important _____ .

6 The police caught the _____ when he tried to sell the jewellery online.

Grammar

4 Complete the sentences with the correct passive form of the verbs in brackets.

1 CCTV cameras _____ (use) in many cities.

2 He _____ (arrest) yesterday for the theft.

3 The stolen money _____ (find) two days after the robbery in the back of a car.

4 A lot of crime _____ (solve) using scientific evidence now.

5 Find and correct the mistakes in the sentences.

1 We need to get our TV repair.
  _____

2 I had my bike stealing.
  _____

3 Shall we get delivered a pizza?
  _____

4 He's having a new suit make.
  _____

6 Complete the sentences with the negative form of the adjectives below. There are two extra words.

> correct   fair   possible   legal   relevant   usual

1 It's _____ to drive before you're old enough.

2 No, that's _____ . It's not the right answer.

3 This is a really difficult case. I think it's _____ to solve!

4 Jack's usually here on time. It's _____ for him to be late.

Speaking language practice

7 Complete the dialogues with the words below.

> don't know   fine   OK   suppose   sure   try   worry

A

A: Tara and I are going to a dance workshop next weekend. Do you want to come?

B: I [1]_____ . I'm not very good at dancing.

A: It'll be [2]_____ . Why don't you [3]_____ ?

B: Yes, you're right. [4]_____ , I'll try. I guess it might be fun!

B

A: I'm really nervous because I've got to sing a song in our next show.

B: Don't [5]_____ ! You've got a lovely voice.

A: Thanks. Well, I [6]_____ I can do it!

B: Yes. I'm [7]_____ you can do it!

1 Match verbs 1–6 with nouns a–f to make word friends.

1	**b** burgle	a	laws
2	☐ chew	b	~~a house~~
3	☐ get	c	gum
4	☐ go to	d	criminals
5	☐ catch	e	a fine
6	☐ pass	f	prison

2 Complete the sentences with the word friends in Exercise 1. Which sentences do you agree with / are true for you?

1 Someone can easily _burgle a house_ if it doesn't have an alarm.
2 It's not enough to _____ for speeding. The driver should be banned.
3 It's not illegal to _____ in my country. I think it's a great habit!
4 In my country, the police don't always _____. There are some unsolved crimes.
5 I think too many people _____ for petty crimes. That's why the prisons are so full these days.
6 We need to _____ all the time because there are lots of new crimes.

3 Choose the correct option.

1 Many people in Iceland leave their bicycles (unlocked) / unstuck.
2 Hong Kong is considered / needed to be one of the safest countries in the world.
3 If you have your bag stolen / robbed, you should call the police.
4 In Finland fines for certain crimes are based / caught on the criminal's income.
5 Chewing gum can get stuck / bought on pavements.
6 You are not happened / allowed to sing on the streets in Hong Kong.

4 Choose the correct option.

1 The underground vault used / (is used) by local diamond dealers.
2 The robbers disconnected / was disconnected all the CCTV cameras, except one.
3 The robber's face hid / was hidden from the camera.
4 The vault located / is located in the basement of the building
5 They brought in the tools that used / were used to get the jewels.
6 They forced / were forced open the security door from inside the lift.
7 It seemed / was seemed to be the perfect crime.
8 The police caught / were caught the robbers in the end.

5 Match pictures A–C with sentences 1–3.

1 ☐ The CCTV images of the robbery were analysed.
2 ☐ The police recorded the robbers' conversations.
3 ☐ The robbers' cars were followed.

6 Complete the sentences with the word friends below.

> big challenge   crime scene   jewellery quarter
> legal history   ~~perfect crime~~   security door

1 The police caught the robbers in the end but it was almost the _perfect crime_.
2 The robbery took place in London's _____.
3 The _____ for the robbers was a fifty-centimetre concrete wall.
4 It is the greatest robbery in Britain's _____.
5 They had to climb down the lift and open the _____.
6 The police presented lots of photos from the _____.

7 Read the video script. Underline any words or phrases you don't know and find their meaning in your dictionary.

A famous robbery

Part 1

In April 2015, just before the long Easter weekend, London's most famous jewellery vault was robbed in a spectacular operation. It seemed like something from a film. Professional robbers stole
5 millions of pounds worth of diamonds from safe deposit boxes which were kept in the vault.

The vault in central London's well-known jewellery quarter is called the Hatton Garden Safe Deposit Company. It was opened in the 1950s and had an underground vault which was used by local
10 diamond dealers to store their jewels. It was considered one of the safest in the country.

On Thursday 2 April 2015, at 21.19, the operation started. The robbers disconnected all the CCTV cameras except one. At 21.23, one robber appeared with a large black sack, but his face was
15 hidden from the camera.

The first challenge was how to get into the vault, which was located in the basement. The robbers had crucial information about this building and worked out that if they could climb down inside the lift, they could eventually enter the vault. They climbed
20 down the inside of the lift using ropes. Then they forced open this security door from the lift. Now they were just one step away from the security boxes with the jewels inside. On the streets above, no one knew that one of the biggest ever robberies was happening.

It was now twenty past midnight, just three hours after the start
25 of the operation. The next big challenge was to drill through the wall of the vault – it was fifty centimeters thick. We tried it out here with some drilling specialists. It took us just two hours and twenty minutes to drill exactly the same holes as the robbers.

Part 2

30 Once inside the vault, they could open the safe deposit boxes. It's easy to do with a simple hammer. Look! You can crack these open in just five minutes!

The police only discovered the robbery two days after the robbers escaped with the jewels, or 'the loot'. Nobody knows how
35 much they escaped with. They were eventually captured by the police six months later. Their downfall was the technology they used. The police were much smarter; they traced their mobile phones, analysed the CCTV images, recorded their conversations and followed their cars. It was the end to an amazing story, to what
40 seemed to be the perfect crime. The police eventually solved the mystery of the largest burglary in English legal history.

9

Think outside the box

VOCABULARY
School subjects | Learning and assessment | Describing students | Phrasal verbs

GRAMMAR
Word order in questions | Mixed tenses

READING
Matching headings to paragraphs | True/False

LISTENING
Identifying specific information | Multiple choice

SPEAKING
Exchanging personal information

WRITING
A letter giving information

B B C CULTURE
Can school be fun?

I can talk about school life.

1 ● Look at the pictures and write the school subjects.

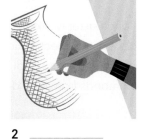

1 _Maths_   2 _____   3 _____

4 _____   5 _____   6 _____

2 ●● Write the correct school subject for each definition.

1 You read books and plays in this subject. **L**_iterature_
2 You learn about the world and different countries in this subject. **G**_____
3 This subject teaches you how to look after your body so you aren't ill. **H**_____
4 In this subject you discuss important ideas, like the meaning of life. **P**_____
5 You need to learn this if you want to visit London. **E**_____
6 You learn about different chemicals in this subject. **C**_____

3 ●● Read the comments and write the school subjects.

1 I think it's important to learn these, so you can talk to people from different countries. _Languages_

2 I really enjoy learning about the law in my country, and how to vote. _____

3 I'm working hard at this subject because I will need it when I go to France next summer. _____

4 I love sport so, of course, this is my favourite subject! _____

5 This is a difficult science subject, but I study it because one day I want to be an astronaut! _____

6 My parents are from Spain so, of course, this subject is really easy for me! _____

4 ● **Choose the correct answers.**

1 I love _____ about how people live in different countries.
   a studying   ⓑ learning   c revising

2 Don't forget: you need to hand in your _____ on Friday.
   a project   b performance
   c practical exam

3 I can't come out tonight. I need to _____ for my Geography test.
   a learn   b revise   c memorise

4 The examiner will ask you questions in the English _____ exam.
   a practical   b performance
   c speaking

5 Are you going to _____ Spanish next year or will you choose a different language?
   a study   b revise
   c memorise

6 We have to produce a drawing for our _____ in Art.
   a performance   b written exam
   c practical exam

5 ●● **Complete the words in the sentences.**

1 I find it difficult to le _a_ _r_n irregular verbs.
2 I usually s___ __y for about an hour every evening.
3 It's difficult to m_m_ _ _ _e a whole poem!
4 I need to r_v_ _e for my Maths exam.
5 We have a p_ _c_ _c_l e_ _ _m in Cookery – we have to cook a meal!
6 For our music exam we have to give a p_ _f_ _m_ _ _e on our instrument.

6 ● **Match 1–5 with a–e to make sentences.**

1 b Someone who is intelligent
2 ☐ Someone who is lazy
3 ☐ Someone who is creative
4 ☐ Someone who is good at teamwork
5 ☐ Someone who is good at general knowledge

a doesn't work hard.
b ~~is very clever and learns quickly.~~
c works well with other people.
d has a good imagination.
e knows a lot of facts about different things.

7 ●●● **Choose the correct words to complete the school web page.**

At Redfield School we believe in a modern approach to education. Of course, students here [1]_____ traditional subjects such as Maths and History, but they also [2]_____ more practical skills, such as [3]_____, which we think are important for life. As well as the main subjects, there are lots of extra classes, such as Yoga and [4]_____ Design. We only have [5]_____ exams once a year and we don't expect students to spend a lot of time [6]_____ for them. We believe that old-fashioned methods of learning such as [7]_____ lots of facts aren't important in the modern world. The internet is there to check facts, so people don't need general [8]_____ in the same way that they did 50 years ago. We believe it's more important to teach our students critical [9]_____ skills so they can form their own opinions. We want our students to be [10]_____ and use their imagination in everything they do. We also believe that [11]_____ is a really important skill, so we encourage our students to work with each other in groups. We are lucky to have a lot of [12]_____ young musicians here, and all our music groups give a [13]_____ to the whole school at the end of each term.

1 a memorise   c perform
   ⓑ study   d revise
2 a learn   c memorise
   b revise   d make
3 a Chemistry   c Cookery
   b Physics   d Philosophy
4 a Photography   c Film
   b Fashion   d Art
5 a writing   c write
   b writer   d written
6 a learning   c performing
   b memorising   d revising
7 a memorising   c revising
   b practising   d getting
8 a facts   c knowledge
   b learning   d understanding
9 a understanding c learning
   b thinking   d knowledge
10 a intelligent   c creative
   b lazy   d gifted
11 a performance   c study
   b teamwork   d problem solving
12 a lazy   c talented
   b practised   d practical
13 a project   c teamwork
   b performance   d practical exam

I can make questions with the correct word order.

1 ● **Choose the correct option.**

1 (Why)/ What is Ted upset?

2 How / When do your exams start?

3 Who / What are you going to invite to your party?

4 What / Where does the performance take place?

5 Where / How did you get home?

2 ● **Order the words to make questions.**

1 you / OK / are / ?
   Are you OK?

2 live / where / you / do / ?
   _____

3 you / book / did / enjoy / the / ?
   _____

4 Sam's / have / met / you / brother / ?
   _____

5 prize / who / the / won / ?
   _____

3 ●● **Read the sentences. Complete the question to fit each answer.**

1 Ellie and Jo *told me about the party*.
   a A: Who told you about the party ?
      B: Ellie and Jo.
   b A: What *did Ellie and Jo tell you about* ?
      B: The party.

2 Sam gave me this card.
   a A: What _____ ?
      B: This card.
   b A: Who _____ ?
      B: Sam.

3 Anna phoned me last night.
   a A: Who _____ ?
      B: Anna.
   b A: Who _____ ?
      B: Me.

4 Tom helped me with my homework.
   a A: What _____ ?
      B: My homework.
   b A: Who _____ ?
      B: Tom.

5 I saw Alex and Tim at the party.
   a A: Who _____ ?
      B: Tim and Alex.
   b A: Where _____ ?
      B: At the party.

4 ●● **Read the answers. Complete the questions.**

1 A: *Is it raining* now?
   B: No, it isn't raining now.

2 A: Where _____ ?
   B: Rosie goes to school in Manchester.

3 A: When _____ ?
   B: The film finished at eight o'clock.

4 A: Who _____ ?
   B: Mrs Cavendish teaches them French.

5 A: Who _____ ?
   B: She phoned Carl.

5 ●●● **Complete the dialogue. Make questions using the words in brackets.**

Rob: Hi, Dad. ¹*What are you doing* (what / you / do)?

Dad: I'm looking at some old photos from school.

Rob: ² _____ (it / be / OK) if I have a look?

Dad: Yes, it's fine.

Rob: ³ _____ (who / take / these photos)?

Dad: I can't remember who took them.

Rob: Wow! It looks very different to my school. ⁴ _____ (what / subjects / you / study)?

Dad: Oh, we studied all the usual subjects.

Rob: ⁵ _____ (you / enjoy / school)?

Dad: Not really. We didn't do many fun activities.

Rob: ⁶ _____ (what / your teachers / be / like)?

Dad: They were very strict!

Rob: ⁷ _____ (who / that / be)?

Dad: My best friend, Tom. We got on really well.

Rob: He looks cool. ⁸ _____ (you / stay / friends) with him since you left school?

Dad: No, I haven't. He went to the USA and I haven't heard from him for years.

6 **Complete the dialogues with the phrases below.**

OUT of **class**

| Good luck!   I hope so. |
| Where do you want it? |

1 A: Oh, is that the new desk for my bedroom?
   B: Yes. _____
   A: Next to the bed, please.

2 A: Are you planning to go to university?
   B: _____ I need to pass all my exams first!

3 A: I've got my French exam tomorrow.
   B: _____ I'm sure you'll do well.

I can find specific detail in an article and talk about intelligence.

1 WORD FRIENDS Complete the sentences with *make* or *take*.

1 We decided to *make* some improvements to the course, so it's much better now.
2 Don't worry if you _____ a mistake in Maths. Just try again and keep trying until you get it right.
3 I'm sure you'll _____ progress in English if you keep working hard.
4 It's a good idea to _____ notes during History lessons so you've got the important facts written down.
5 I don't understand this sentence – it doesn't _____ sense!
6 We have to _____ an exam in the summer to check that we understand everything we've learned.
7 There are some things we're not happy with at the school, so we'd like to _____ a few changes.
8 Come and _____ a look at this photo – it's really funny!

2 Read the article. Match headings a–d with paragraphs 1–4.

a What are the advantages of homeschooling?
b Facts and figures about homeschooling
c Do homeschoolers get good results?
d Are there any disadvantages?

3 Read the text again. Mark the sentences T (true) or F (false).

1 ☐ Homeschooling is possible in every country.
2 ☐ A study in Britain showed that homeschoolers are more successful than students at school.
3 ☐ Fran likes being in control of her studies.
4 ☐ Adam thinks he gets more attention now that he is homeschooled.
5 ☐ Homeschoolers are always lonely because they don't have a large group of friends.

4 Complete the sentences with the correct form of the highlighted phrases from the text.

1 You should *make a real effort* to learn English vocabulary.
2 Winning this money will _____ to our lives.
3 Sara's very independent and doesn't enjoy _____ from other people.
4 It's difficult to _____ between the two films, because they're so different.

Learning at home

1 _____

Would you prefer to stay at home to study? In many countries it is compulsory for children to attend school. In Britain, children have a legal right to an education, but it doesn't have to take place in a school. Parents can choose to teach their children at home. Around 36,000 students are currently homeschooled in Britain, and the number is growing.

2 _____

It's difficult to make comparisons between the achievements of homeschooled students and those of students at school. However, studies in the USA, where homeschooling is more popular, have shown that students educated at home often achieve better results in national tests than those in school. In Britain homeschooled students regularly get places at top universities.

3 _____

Most homeschoolers speak very positively of their experiences. Fran, fifteen, enjoys having the freedom to spend more time on subjects she likes. 'At school, there's a set programme of study that all students have to follow. I don't have to take instructions from teachers. I can follow my own interests more and explore subjects in more depth.' Adam, fourteen, also sees benefits to homeschooling. 'Teachers in schools have thirty students to think about. I have a tutor just for me. I love the fact that I can ask lots of questions, and he can really help me to understand things. That makes a big difference to me.'

4 _____

People often assume that the biggest problem for homeschoolers is loneliness. In fact, this isn't the case. Most parents of homeschoolers make a real effort to create a network of friends for their children, and they often end up having quite interesting social lives. However, psychologists warn that some students who are homeschooled may have difficulties later in life. Dr Rob Alexander says, 'School isn't just about education – it's about learning to fit in. At school, students learn teamwork, and they learn how to deal with a wide range of different personalities. You can't get that at home.'

I can use a variety of tenses.

1 ● **Complete the sentences with the verbs below. There are two extra verbs.**

> didn't have   haven't had   left   'm going to go
> 'm seeing   plays   's playing   ~~were living~~

1 My parents *were living* in London when I was born.
2 I _____ Tom tomorrow evening, so I can ask him about the project then.
3 We _____ our exam results yet. I hope I've done well!
4 Jack's upstairs at the moment – I think he _____ computer games.
5 My brother _____ school last year and now he's looking for a job.
6 I _____ online tonight, to find some information for my project.

2 ●● **Complete the sentences with the correct form of the verbs below. Use the Present Simple, Present Continuous or Present Perfect.**

> break   change   listen   love   ~~study~~   try

1 What *are* you *studying* in Biology at the moment?
2 A lot of things _____ at our school in the last two years – it's very different now!
3 Dan never _____ to the teacher, so he doesn't know what homework to do.
4 Be quiet – I _____ to revise!
5 Amy isn't at school today because she _____ her leg.
6 I _____ Maths – it's my favourite subject!

3 ●● **Read some students' excuses for not doing their homework. Complete them with the correct form of the verbs in brackets. Use the Past Simple or Past Continuous.**

I ¹*fell* (fall) asleep while I ²_____ (watch) TV. While I ³_____ (sleep), my dog ⁴_____ (take) my homework outside and ⁵_____ (bury) it in the garden.

I ⁶_____ (spill) water on my school bag while I ⁷_____ (help) my mum in the kitchen. Unfortunately, all my books ⁸_____ (get) wet!

The school bus ⁹_____ (arrive) early this morning, while I ¹⁰_____ (have) breakfast. I ¹¹_____ (leave) the house quickly and I ¹²_____ (forget) my homework. Sorry!

4 ●● **Choose the correct option.**

1 I'm sure you (will get)/ *are getting* good marks in your exams next week.
2 How many people *are you going to / do you* invite to the party next month?
3 Hurry up – the train *leaves / will leave* in five minutes!
4 Do you want to come to the cinema with us this evening? We *will meet / are meeting* outside the cinema at 6.30.
5 I think that in the future students *are studying / will study* at home more.
6 What *are you going to do / do you do* to celebrate the end of exams next week?

5 ●●● **Complete the article with the correct form of the verbs in brackets.**

The world's biggest school

The City of Montessori School in Lucknow, India, ¹*holds* (hold) the world record for the world's largest school, with over 50,000 students! The school first ²_____ (open) in 1959, with only five students. Dr Jagdish Gandhi, the founder of the school, says it was difficult to get students at first. He and his wife ³_____ (work) very hard in the first few years while they ⁴_____ (try) to achieve their dream of a good school for their city. The school ⁵_____ (grow) a lot since those early days. It now ⁶_____ (employ) 3,800 teachers, and lessons ⁷_____ (take place) at twenty different sites across the city. And it ⁸_____ (still / grow)! The next school year ⁹_____ (start) in June, and who knows how many students there ¹⁰_____ (be) by that time!

I can identify specific information in a dialogue and talk about awkward moments.

1 Complete the sentences with the correct form of the phrasal verbs below.

> calm down   fill in   get on   hand in   hand out   look over   look up   ~~mess about~~

1 Archie shouldn't *mess about* in class all the time – he needs to work harder.
2 The teacher wants us to _____ our projects on Friday, but I haven't started mine yet!
3 Remember to leave time at the end of the exam to _____ all your answers.
4 _____ ! There's nothing to be upset or angry about.
5 I keep my dictionary with me so I can _____ words that I don't know.
6 It's time to stop playing computer games and _____ with your homework!
7 You have to _____ a form to join the gym.
8 Tanya, please _____ these books – one to every pair of students.

2 🔊 29 Listen to some people talking about school life. Choose the correct answers.

1 What did the teacher catch the girl doing in class?

 **A**    **B**    **C**

2 Who did the boy write a text to?

 **A**    **B**    **C**

3 Why is the girl late for school?

 **A**    **B**    **C**

4 What happened to the boy at the ceremony?

 **A**    **B**    **C**

5 What has the girl lost?

 **A**    **B**    **C**

3 🔊 30 Choose the correct answers. Listen and check.

1 Have you all finished the first exercise?
   a Yes, we are.
   b Not quite, Sir.
   c No, we didn't.

2 Did you manage to answer all the questions in the test?
   a No, I didn't.
   b Yes, we have.
   c No, they aren't.

3 Could you lend me a pen, please?
   a No, I don't.
   b Yes, I have.
   c Of course.

4 How long did you spend on your Maths homework?
   a About an hour.
   b No, I didn't spend any.
   c For half an hour.

I can have a casual conversation.

1 Complete the questions with the words below.

| are | ~~been~~ | do | have |
| was | would |

1 How have you *been* ?
2 What _____ you guys doing this evening?
3 _____ you like it here?
4 How _____ your journey?
5 _____ you been to the USA before?
6 _____ you like to join us?

2 Choose the correct responses.

1 Have you been to London before?
   a Yes, I did.
   b I didn't go to London.
   c No, it's my first time here.

2 Would you like to come out with us?
   a I'd love to.
   b No, I don't, thanks.
   c Yes, I love it.

3 What are you doing at the weekend?
   a I didn't enjoy it.
   b I'm fine, thanks.
   c I'm going to a party.

4 Do you like it here in New York?
   a Thanks, that would be great.
   b Yes, it's amazing.
   c I'd love to.

5 How was your journey?
   a It was fine.
   b Sure thing.
   c Not really.

3 Complete the dialogues with the phrases below.

OUT of class

| Great to see you! | I'm shattered. |
| ~~Let me introduce you.~~ | Tell me about it! |

1 A: Who's that over there?
   B: That's Liam. *Let me introduce you.* You'll get on well with him.

2 A: Hi, Rob.
   B: Hi, Matt. _____ You look well. Did you have a good holiday?

3 A: I've got loads of homework this week!
   B: _____ I spent two hours on my Maths homework last night!

4 A: Hi, Jodie. How was your journey?
   B: It was awful! The train was two hours late! _____
   A: Well, never mind. You're here now, so you can relax.

4 🔊 31 Complete the dialogues with one word in each gap. Listen and check.

Elsa: Hi, Rory.

Rory: Hi, Elsa. Great to ¹*see* you! Come in.

Elsa: I'm sorry I'm a bit late.

Rory: Oh, don't worry about that. How ²_____ your journey?

Elsa: Not brilliant! The train was really crowded. I ³_____ feeling really tired.

Rory: Well, sit down and I'll get you a cup of tea.

Elsa: Thanks. Your room's nice. ⁴_____ you like it here?

Rory: Yeah. The university's great and I've made lots of friends. How about you? ⁵_____ have you been?

Elsa: Oh, fine. We all miss you back home, of course. I can't wait to get away to college next year!

Later ...

Elsa: It's nice to sit down!

Rory: Yeah. I often come here for a snack.

Elsa: It's nice. Ooh, that chocolate cake looks good.

Rory: Oh, there's Tara – a friend of mine. ⁶_____ me introduce you. Tara – over here!

Tara: Hi.

Rory: Tara, this is Elsa. She's a friend of mine from back home.

Tara: Nice to meet you, Elsa. ⁷_____ you been to Edinburgh before?

Elsa: No, I haven't. But it's a lovely city.

Tara: Yeah. I love it. So, what are you guys ⁸_____ this evening?

Rory: We're going for a pizza. ⁹_____ you like to join us?

Tara: I'd love to. Thanks!

I can write a letter giving information.

1 Read Ana's letter. Complete it with the words below.

> arriving looking meet ~~thank~~ will

2 Read Fiona's reply. Match sentences 1–6 from Fiona's letter with functions a–f.

1 | b | It was good to hear from you.
2 | ☐ | Call me if you can't see us!
3 | ☐ | You wanted to know about my town.
4 | ☐ | There are lots of interesting old buildings.
5 | ☐ | We're going to have a great time!
6 | ☐ | See you soon!

a ending your letter
b ~~starting your letter~~
c before you finish
d making arrangements
e giving useful information
f making it clear why you're writing

3 Complete Fiona's letter with the correct phrases.

> don't worry about   if you like
> ~~I'm looking forward to meeting you~~
> you're welcome to come along
> just in case

4 Write a reply to Ana's letter in Exercise 1. Follow the instructions below.

1 Use Fiona's letter in Exercise 2 as a model.

2 Follow these steps:
   - Start your letter with a suitable phrase.
   - Make it clear why you're writing.
   - Answer all Ana's questions.
   - Give useful information about your town.
   - Make arrangements to meet Ana.
   - Use a friendly phrase before you finish.
   - End your letter with a suitable phrase.

Hi Fiona,

¹<u>Thank</u> you for inviting me to come and visit you. I'm ² _____ next Saturday evening. My plane lands at 7.30. ³_____ you come and meet me at the airport? I'll wear my red coat so you can see me easily. 😊

I'm ⁴_____ forward to seeing your town. Is it old or modern? Are there lots of interesting things to do? I like visiting museums. Also, I love shopping. Are there any good shopping centres in your town?

It will be good to ⁵_____ you at last.

Ana

Hi Ana,

It was good to hear from you.
¹<u>**I'm looking forward to meeting you**</u> too.
Yes, my mum's going to drive me to the airport to meet you. I'm sure I'll recognise you from your photo. My phone number is 07702 354276, ² _____ there's a problem. Call me if you can't see us!
You wanted to know about my town. Well, it's very old. There are lots of interesting old buildings and there's also a great museum about the history of the town. We can visit it while you're here ³ _____. I go to a drama class on Saturday mornings. ⁴ _____ and join in. I'm glad you like shopping. There's a really big shopping centre in my town, with lots of amazing shops. I go there quite a lot – I love shopping too, so we'll definitely do that!
⁵ _____ anything. We're going to have a great time!
See you soon!
Fiona

9.8 **SELF-ASSESSMENT**

For each learning objective, tick (✓) the box that best matches your ability.

😊😊 = I understand and can help a friend.   ☹ = I understand but have some questions.

😊 = I understand and can do it by myself.   ☹☹ = I do not understand.

		😊😊	😊	☹	☹☹	Need help?	Now try ...
9.1	Vocabulary					Students' Book pp. 106–107 Workbook pp. 102–103	Ex. 1–3, p. 111
9.2	Grammar					Students' Book p. 108 Workbook p. 104	Ex. 4–5, p. 111
9.3	Reading					Students' Book p. 109 Workbook p. 105	
9.4	Grammar					Students' Book p. 110 Workbook p. 106	Ex. 6, p. 111
9.5	Listening					Students' Book p. 111 Workbook p. 107	
9.6	Speaking					Students' Book p. 112 Workbook p. 108	Ex. 7, p. 111
9.7	Writing					Students' Book p. 113 Workbook p. 109	

9.1   I can talk about school life.
9.2   I can make questions with the correct word order.
9.3   I can find specific detail in an article and talk about intelligence.
9.4   I can use a variety of tenses.
9.5   I can identify specific information in a dialogue and talk about awkward moments.
9.6   I can have a casual conversation.
9.7   I can write a letter giving information.

What can you remember from this unit?

New words I learned (the words you most want to remember from this unit)	**Expressions and phrases I liked** (any expressions or phrases you think sound nice, useful or funny)	**English I heard or read outside class** (e.g. from websites, books, adverts, films, music)

Vocabulary

1 Match the words below with the definitions.

| ICT Literature Maths performance practical exam project |

1 a school subject in which you learn about numbers _____
2 a test in which you make something rather than answer questions _____
3 a school subject in which you learn about computers _____
4 a situation in which you do something on a stage for other people to watch

_____
5 a school subject in which you learn about novels, plays and poems _____
6 a piece of work in which you study and write about a topic in detail _____

2 Choose the correct option.

1 What's the best way to *revise* / *memorise* for exams?
2 You must *memorise* / *study* this number so that you can remember it.
3 We're *studying* / *learning* about plants in Biology at the moment.
4 You won't do well in your exams if you're *lazy* / *creative*.
5 Come and *make* / *take* a look at this picture.
6 You need to *fill in* / *calm down* this form.

3 Complete the sentences with the words below. There are two extra words.

| critical general mess mistakes photography problem talented teamwork |

1 Max is really good at _____ solving, so I'll ask him what we should do.
2 Simon doesn't like working on his own – he prefers _____.
3 No, I don't know the capital of Hungary – my _____ knowledge isn't very good.
4 We did some exercises to develop our _____ thinking skills.
5 I made a lot of _____ in my English test, so I don't think I'll pass.
6 You won't do well at school if you _____ around in class.

Grammar

4 Complete the questions with the correct form of the verbs in brackets.

1 _____ (your friends/go) shopping every weekend?
2 _____ (you/finish) reading that book yet?
3 _____ (why/Carrie/be) upset today?
4 _____ (who/call) the police last night?
5 _____ (who/you/see) at the cinema yesterday?

5 Match answers a–e with questions 1–5 in Exercise 4.

a ☐ Because she failed her Chemistry exam.
b ☐ I saw Tim and Mel.
c ☐ Yes, I have.
d ☐ Yes, they do.
e ☐ Marty called them.

6 Choose the correct option.

1 *I play* / *I'm playing* tennis every weekend.
2 Someone *stole* / *was stealing* my bike yesterday.
3 We *walked* / *were walking* home when we saw him.
4 The school *became* / *has become* very popular over the last few years.
5 Do yoga. It *is helping* / *will help* you to stay flexible.
6 The new term *starts* / *is going to start* in two weeks.

Speaking language practice

7 Complete the dialogues with the phrases below.

| do you like have you been how have how was would you like what are |

A
A: Hi, Laura. Great to see you after so long!
¹_____ you been?
B: Fine.
A: Your flat's really nice. ²_____ it here?
B: Yes, I love it!

B
A: Hi, nice to see you. ³_____ your journey?
B: Not bad. Not too tiring.
A: Good. ⁴_____ to Manchester before?
B: No, I haven't. I'm looking forward to seeing it.

C
A: Hi. ⁵_____ you guys doing tonight?
B: We're meeting some friends at the cinema.
⁶_____ to join us?
A: Thanks. I'd love to.

1 Match words 1–6 with words a–f to make word friends from the text. How many other word friends can you make?

1	f research	a	facts
2	☐ memorise	b	your potential
3	☐ take	c	it in turns
4	☐ achieve	d	pictures
5	☐ draw	e	the material
6	☐ revise	f	the topic

2 Complete the sentences with the word friends in Exercise 1.

1 If you are doing a project, it's a good idea to *research the topic* well.

2 Before an exam, you usually have to _____ that you have studied in class.

3 Our teacher is very creative – she makes us _____ and make models of the subject we are studying.

4 Some teachers say that you shouldn't just _____ , but try to understand them.

5 We _____ to give presentations – that means everybody gets a chance.

6 A good teacher should encourage you to _____ .

3 Complete the text with the words below. There are two extra words.

| potential | ~~positive~~ | academic | alternative |
| fascinating | critical | interactive | |

Adam has a very ¹*positive* attitude towards his school. He is a very practical person and he likes the fact that they spend less time on ² _____ subjects. He realises that the system is ³ _____ , but he prefers it to the traditional school model. For him, the ⁴ _____ element is very important – he likes working together with others. He also likes the choice. For example, he spoke about a presentation he did on allergies, which was a ⁵ _____ topic for him.

4 Match the phrases below with the photos. Write sentences in the Present Continuous. There are two extra phrases.

| do martial arts | ~~shake hands~~ | stand in playground |
| study Computer Science | study English | do Drama |

1 *The teacher is shaking hands with the student.*

2 _____

3 _____

4 _____

5 Choose the correct option.

1 At King's School the students have very (high) / little expectations.

2 At King's School they teach a course in *public* / *private* speaking.

3 At Steiner schools the atmosphere is more *informal* / *ordered*.

4 Shapwick is a *private* / *formal* school for children with dyslexia.

5 Dyslexia can affect people's *old-fashioned* / *short-term* memory.

6 Complete the sentences with the words below.

| atmosphere | discipline | fees | full-time | ~~values~~ |

1 Some schools have *values* that they want to maintain, like being a good citizen.

2 If you want to go to a private school, you have to pay _____ .

3 King's School prepares students for life after _____ education.

4 There is a different _____ in the Steiner schools – it's very relaxed.

5 At the King's School there is more emphasis on _____ and obeying orders.

7 Read the video script. Underline any words or phrases you don't know and find their meaning in your dictionary.

Two very different schools

Part 1

Narrator: Lunchtime over at King's and the playground becomes a parade ground. King's opened as a free school in 2012 and now has 280 pupils in three year groups. Each lesson begins with a handshake for the teacher and a statement
5 of the school's values. This brings a feeling of order and discipline to the class. This is a Leadership class. The subject today is integrity.

Interviewer: Wouldn't this time be better spent teaching the pupils Maths or English or Science?

Teacher: It's these kinds of lessons that enable the students to do as well as they do
10 in subjects like Maths and English and Science because it teaches them 'character'.

Narrator: All students at King's have to do martial arts.

Interviewer: The insistence on order and character-building will sound old-fashioned to some. So, is this a deliberate attempt to turn back the clock?

15 Narrator: They teach Latin and Public Speaking here, but they also teach Mandarin and Computer Science. The children are encouraged to have high expectations.

Girl: I want to be an investment banker and to do… to go to Oxford University.

Interviewer: How old are you now?

Girl: I'm thirteen.

20 Narrator: The government also recognises the good work at King's school and hopes other schools will follow. At Kings, they believe they are doing something new: preparing their students for life after full-time education.
The King's free school is very different from the Steiner school system.
Here, discipline and exams are not the priority and there is a very informal
25 atmosphere. Students don't wear a uniform and don't start academic studies until they are seven. The focus is on creative play, music, drama and dance.

Part 2

Narrator: Another kind of alternative school is one that focuses on special needs. In the UK there are fourteen schools which specialise in teaching dyslexic children. Our
30 reporter, Kara – a dyslexic herself, talks about her visit to one of these schools.

Kara: I'm really kind of excited about seeing a school that specialises in something that I've had throughout my life.

Narrator: Shapwick is a private school with 170 boys and girls. The classes are very small, so the teacher can focus on the needs of particular students. The first class that
35 Kara attends is an English lesson.
Dyslexia doesn't just affect reading and spelling. It can also affect your short-term memory. Here, students learn new words by linking them to colours, shapes and stories. This makes it easier for them to remember the new words. The students are very hard-working.
40 Most dyslexic schoolchildren don't get this support. Schools like Shapwick are expensive and many parents cannot afford the fees. However, some families are given money by the government.
As part of their English lesson, the children spell out words with physical movements. Here, they are using bottles of water. It helps the words to stay in
45 their long-term memory. Kara didn't have the chance to study this way when she was a girl, but she's very happy that now others can.

1 Look at the text in each question. What does it say? Choose the correct letter a, b or c.

Tip: Read each text carefully and think about its purpose and general meaning. Then read the three options and choose the one that matches.

Example:

1
Special offer today!
Free ice cream with every pizza!

a There is a special price for ice cream today.

ⓑ When you buy a pizza, you can have an ice cream without paying.

c Pizzas are free today.

2
No selfie sticks in the museum, except in the entrance hall

a You can buy selfie sticks in the entrance hall.

b You can't use selfie sticks anywhere in the museum.

c You can use selfie sticks in the entrance hall, but nowhere else.

3
Hi Tara! Can you lend me your phone charger? I can't find mine and I need to charge my phone. I can come and get it this afternoon if you're at home. I promise to return it tomorrow! Elsie

a Elsie is asking Tara to bring the charger to her house.

b Elsie wants to borrow Tara's charger.

c Elsie wants to come to Tara's house to use her charger.

4
Danger – risk of death or serious injury
This part of the mountain is closed to skiers due to the risk of avalanches.

a You can't ski here because there's the possibility of an avalanche.

b Some skiers have already died or been injured on the mountain.

c People should be careful when they are skiing here because there has been an avalanche.

5
Tom,
It's my birthday party on Saturday.
I hope you haven't forgotten.
Come round at seven as we agreed.
Remember to bring my present!
Alan

Why has Alan written this note?

a to invite Tom to his birthday party

b to arrange with Tom what time he should come

c to remind Tom about his party

6
PHONE MESSAGE
To: Paul   **From:** The Pizza Place
The pizza restaurant phoned. They've made a mistake with their bookings, so your table is now for 7.30 p.m., not 7.00 p.m. Ring back if the later time is a problem.

Paul should call the restaurant

a to confirm that the new booking is OK.

b if he isn't happy with the new booking.

c to tell them about a mistake.

2 These people all want to find a place to eat. On the next page are descriptions of eight restaurants. Decide which restaurant (A–H) would be the most suitable for each person (1–5).

Tip: Read about each person carefully and underline the important points. Then read each description and find the one that matches all the important points.

1 ☐ Becky is looking for somewhere to spend an evening with a big group of friends to celebrate her sixteenth birthday. She and her friends don't have much money, and three of them are vegetarians.

2 ☐ Neil wants to take his wife out for a quiet evening meal to celebrate their tenth wedding anniversary. They both enjoy traditional well-cooked dishes. They don't particularly like spicy food.

3 ☐ Jane is having a day shopping with some college friends and is looking for a place to stop off on the way home for a drink and a snack. She particularly likes sweet things.

4 ☐ Helen wants to take her two ten-year-old nephews out for lunch for a birthday treat. They're very lively and they aren't happy unless they have something to do. They especially love computer games. They don't eat much and they're quite fussy eaters.

5 ☐ Dan and his school friends want a quick lunch before they go to the cinema. They want something light and not expensive. The restaurant must be in the city centre so it's close to the cinema.

Restaurant guide

A Joe's Diner

Definitely sells the best burgers in town. The steaks are great too, with delicious handmade chips. It's popular with students, although others might not like the loud music and bright lights. It isn't cheap and there isn't much choice unless you like steak or burgers! The portions are also too big for most people to finish.

B The Shed

Located twenty minutes from the city centre, this lunchtime-only restaurant is big and busy. You order your food on tablet computers at the table, which is fun, and you can play on the tablet while you wait for your food. There's plenty of choice and the menu is mix and match, so you can choose exactly what you want.

C Mexicana

Mexicana offers top quality Mexican and South American food in a relaxed atmosphere. The look is traditional, but the food is definitely modern, created by a chef who loves experimenting. The dishes are full of new and exciting flavours, most with a generous helping of chilli! Prices are high, and it's small, so you need to book well in advance.

D Pizza Plus

A great value restaurant serving pizzas and pasta dishes which are tasty and not expensive. There's plenty of choice, including vegetable-only options. There's live music most nights and the restaurant, which is quite big, is usually full of young people, so there's often a real party atmosphere. The only problem is that the service can be slow.

E The Vegetable Garden

If you're looking for modern vegetarian cooking at its best, The Vegetable Garden is the restaurant for you. All the dishes use fresh local ingredients and many of the vegetables are grown in the restaurant's garden. There are tasty bean dishes and the noodles are fantastic! Prices are quite high and it's only open at lunch times.

F La Rustique

This small French restaurant is elegant and relaxing. The tables are arranged to give you a feeling of privacy and there's an excellent selection of well-known dishes from Coq au Vin to Boeuf Bourguignon – classic French food at its best. It's expensive, but it's well worth the money for a special occasion.

G Temptations

This city centre café is open all day, serving drinks and snacks. There are some unusual drinks like strawberry lemonade, and there's an amazing range of fresh fruit juices too. The best thing is the delicious homemade cakes and ice creams – try the chocolate and coconut cake! Service can be a bit slow, but it's worth the wait!

H Dario's

This lively café is right in the city centre. The reasonable prices make it popular, especially with students and young people. The evening menu isn't particularly exciting, but at lunch time there's a great selection of tasty soups, fresh salads and some unusual sandwiches. Service is quick too.

3 Read the text and choose the correct letter (a, b, c or d) for each space.

Tip: Read the text through quickly for general meaning first. Then focus on each gap. Look carefully at the words before and after each gap and see which of the four options fits best.

WILD PLACES

More and more people now ¹_____ visiting wild places for their holidays. Trips to hot deserts or ²_____ cold northern countries are becoming more and more popular. A lot of places that were ³_____ difficult to get to in the past are now only a plane ride away. Scientists too are studying the wild places of the world, hoping to ⁴_____ new and unusual plants and animals. Of course, tourists who visit these places ⁵_____ their best not to cause any damage and they certainly don't ⁶_____ to harm the natural world. They just want to experience the natural beauty of the places and take photos that they can ⁷_____ with their friends. But is tourism killing these wild places that we love so much? They have remained in a natural state ⁸_____ thousands of years. Do we really ⁹_____ to change this and turn them into holiday resorts? So, before you ¹⁰_____ the decision to go to one of the world's wild places, maybe you should stop and think. If you haven't been there ¹¹_____, maybe it's best to stay away.

Example:

	a		b		c		d	
1	a	choose	ⓑ	enjoy	c	decide	d	hope
2	a	cool	b	chilly	c	freezing	d	mild
3	a	really	b	completely	c	absolutely	d	totally
4	a	look	b	discover	c	have	d	find out
5	a	make	b	put	c	do	d	attempt
6	a	realise	b	think	c	mean	d	enjoy
7	a	show	b	bring	c	upload	d	share
8	a	for	b	since	c	before	d	ago
9	a	like	b	stand	c	want	d	accept
10	a	do	b	get	c	have	d	make
11	a	never	b	yet	c	ever	d	just

4 For each question, complete the second sentence so that it means the same as the first. Use no more than three words.

Tip: Read the first sentence carefully, to make sure you understand the meaning in detail. Then read the second sentence and think of another way of expressing the same meaning.

Example:

1 Mike phoned me a few second ago.
  Mike has _just phoned_ me.
2 I'm happy to help with the cooking.
  I don't _____ helping with the cooking.
3 Martha can play tennis really well.
  Martha is really good _____ tennis.
4 This is the first time I've eaten pineapple ice cream.
  I've _____ pineapple ice cream before.
5 My dad started working there in 2014.
  My dad has worked _____ 2014.
6 I'm afraid there's nothing for dessert.
  I'm afraid there isn't _____ for dessert.

5 You borrowed your friend Sam's headphones, but you have lost them. Write an email to Sam. In your email, you should:

• apologise to Sam.
• explain to Sam where and when you lost them.
• offer to buy Sam some new headphones.

Write **35–45 words.**

Tip: You must include all the three points that are mentioned in the task.

6 Read the exam task. What two questions should you answer and how many words should you write?

> This is part of a letter you receive from an English friend:
>
> For a piece of homework, I have to find out about weather and natural disasters in another country. What's the weather like in your country? Have there been any natural disasters? Write and tell me!
>
> Now write a letter answering your friend's questions. Write your letter in about 100 words.

7 Write the words below in the correct column.

> ~~autumn~~ avalanche cloudy drought earthquake flood fog hurricane icy rainy snow spring storm summer sunny tsunami wind winter

Seasons	Weather nouns
autumn	_____
_____	_____
_____	_____
Weather adjectives	**Natural disasters**
_____	_____
_____	_____
_____	_____
_____	_____
	_____
	_____

8 Match 1–6 with a–f to make sentences.

1 [b] Let me know
2 [ ] Anyway, good luck with
3 [ ] Dear
4 [ ] Thanks for getting
5 [ ] Bye for
6 [ ] Great to hear

a from you. [ ]
b ~~how you get on with your homework.~~ [E]
c now. [ ]
d your homework. [ ]
e in touch. [ ]
f Sam, ... [ ]

9 Read the sentences in Exercise 8 and decide if you would use them at the beginning (B) or end (E) of a letter.

10 Write your answer to the exam task in Exercise 6.

1 Look at the text in each question. What does it say? Choose the correct letter a, b or c.

Tip: All three options may use vocabulary from the text. Read each of the options very carefully to see which one exactly matches the purpose or meaning of the text.

Example:

> **1**
> ## Special offer today!
> ### Free ice cream with every pizza!

a There is a special price for ice cream today.

(b) When you buy a pizza, you can have an ice cream without paying.

c Pizzas are free today.

> **2**
> Hi Jan! Jamie has just texted me. He's got two tickets for *Mama Mia* next Saturday, but he can't go now, so he wants to sell them. Are you interested? If so, we have to let him know today. Sara

Sara and Jan need to

a go to the theatre to buy tickets for *Mama Mia*.

b tell Jamie if they have any tickets for *Mama Mia*.

c tell Jamie if they want to buy his tickets for *Mama Mia*.

> **3**
> ## Ticket holders only
> All fans must show their tickets at the gate to gain entry to the stadium. Our staff may also ask you for identification.

a You can't buy a ticket unless you show some form of identification.

b You need a ticket to get in and you might need to show some form of identification.

c You can buy tickets at the gate.

> **4**
> ## Essay Competition
> **Subject:** *My best travel experience*
> Entries must be no more than 400 words and must have an accompanying photo.
> **Closing date:** *20 June*

a You have to write more than 400 words.

b You have to send a photo and a piece of writing.

c You don't have to send a photo with your essay.

> **5**
> Matt,
> I left my football boots in the changing room after the match on Saturday. Are you going to the sports centre later? Could you see if they're there? I hope no one's taken them!
> Duncan

Why has Duncan written this note?

a to ask Matt to look for his football boots

b to ask if he can borrow Matt's football boots

c to ask Matt if he has found his football boots

> **6**
> GUESTS SHOULD NOT LEAVE MONEY OR VALUABLE ITEMS IN THEIR TENTS WHEN THEY LEAVE THE CAMPSITE.
>
> YOU CAN LEAVE THESE ITEMS AT THE RECEPTION DESK FOR A SMALL CHARGE, BUT YOU MUST COLLECT THEM BEFORE 8 P.M.

a Guests must always take valuable items with them when they go off the campsite.

b Guests can only collect their valuable items from the reception desk after 8 p.m.

c Guests have to pay to leave valuable items at the reception desk.

2 Look at the sentences about a trip to India. **Read the text to decide if each sentence is correct (C) or incorrect (I).**

Tip: Read the sentences first, then read the text quickly for general meaning. Find the relevant part of the text for each sentence and read that part carefully to see if the sentence is correct or incorrect.

1 ☐ It was Jake's idea to go to India with his dad.

2 ☐ Jake felt excited and slightly anxious before the holiday.

3 ☐ India didn't feel very different to Jake when he first arrived.

4 ☐ Jake preferred the hotel in Delhi to the one in Jaipur.

5 ☐ Jake became bored with visiting historic buildings in Jaipur.

6 ☐ Jake found the train journey to the south uncomfortable and disappointing.

7 ☐ According to Jake, travelling by car can be frightening at times.

8 ☐ Jake was annoyed that he didn't see any tigers in the wildlife park.

9 ☐ Jake was glad that they ignored the warnings about food in the guidebook.

10 ☐ Jake and his dad said they would return to India one day.

A trip to India

by Jake Davis

My dad has always wanted to go to India, but my mum has never been particularly interested in visiting the country. So last year my dad decided to take me there for a three-week holiday. Although I was looking forward to the trip, I was also a bit nervous about visiting a country with such a different culture.

We landed in Delhi and as we drove out of the airport, I could see immediately that it was not at all like home. The first thing that struck me was how many people there were – there were people everywhere, on bikes and motorbikes, pushing handcarts or walking with large bundles on their heads. Everywhere I turned, there were different sights, sounds and smells.

We spent two days exploring Delhi before moving on to Jaipur, a smaller city that is known for its famous pink-coloured buildings. I enjoyed our stay here in a typical Indian hotel. This was much nicer than the big international hotel where we had stayed in Delhi. I felt I was really in India now! We spent two days visiting monuments and palaces in and around Jaipur, which, although interesting at first, became less so after the fifth or sixth one!

After Jaipur, we took a long train journey south to Kerala in a train packed with people, animals and all kinds of goods. Travelling by train in India is definitely an interesting experience, but not as enjoyable as I expected, and the heat was almost unbearable. Travelling by car with an experienced local driver is much more enjoyable, although at times you want to close your eyes when your driver speeds past a red light, beeping his horn loudly to warn other traffic that he's coming!

In our final week we visited a large wildlife park. Although the advertisement promised us tigers, the closest we came to seeing one was a rather old-looking paw print on the ground. This didn't matter though, as we saw elephants and were lucky enough to spot a family of these animals in a river, the young ones splashing around playfully. This more than made up for the lack of tigers!

All in all, the holiday was a wonderful experience. The food was definitely one of the highlights. We enjoyed some wonderful hot snacks from food stalls by the side of the road, despite the advice in the guidebooks to only eat in hotels and restaurants. The other thing I will really remember from the trip is the kindness and warmth of the people. As Dad and I boarded the plane to come home, we promised ourselves that it wouldn't be the last time we would see this amazing country.

3 Read the text and questions below. For each question (1–5), choose the correct letter, a, b, c or d.

Tip: Read the whole text through for general meaning first. Some questions ask about details of the text, so you need to find the relevant part for each one and read it carefully. Some questions ask about the writer's purpose or attitude. For these questions, think about the general meaning of the whole text.

The circus
by Emma Jenkins

People often ask me what it's like to be a circus performer. I grew up in a circus family, so I've always watched the performances and I never questioned the fact that I would grow up to be part of the show.

I decided when I was four years old that I wanted to be a trapeze artist with my cousins, flying through the air high above everyone's head. I wanted to start training immediately, but my parents thought I was too young. A year later, I was playing with my cousins and they showed me a few basic skills. They quickly saw that I was a natural performer, so they persuaded my parents to allow me to start training, even though I was still young.

Although I love performing and each day brings something different, it isn't all fun. For a start, we move to a new place every two weeks. This isn't as tiring as it sounds because we get time off to rest during the day, but it means that it isn't easy to meet new people and form friendships. Of course, our family members are also our friends, and it's great to train, perform and live with the same people.

I don't go to school, but my mum gives me lessons and I also study on my own. Although it's hard to find the time, I know that I need to be disciplined because it's just as important as my performing career. After all, I may need to find a different job one day.

I know that my life is unusual, and it was something I was born to, not something that I chose. I sometimes think about doing something different, but somehow the daily routine of training and performing is in my blood, and I find it impossible to think of anything I would enjoy more.

1 What is Emma trying to do in this text?
   a persuade other people to become circus performers
   b explain why she chose to join a circus
   c suggest how to become a circus performer
   d describe her life as a circus performer

2 Emma started training when
   a she was four years old.
   b her parents persuaded her that she was old enough.
   c she realised she needed to learn some basic skills.
   d her cousins saw how talented she was.

3 What does Emma not enjoy about her way of life?
   a Travelling around a lot is very tiring.
   b It's difficult to make new friends.
   c It can be boring to do the same show every day.
   d It can be difficult working and living with the same people.

4 How does Emma feel about her education?

   a She doesn't think it's necessary for her to have an education.

   b She would like to go to school to learn.

   c She doesn't have much time for school work, but she knows it is necessary.

   d She thinks it's more important to concentrate on her career in the circus.

5 What might Emma say about her life?

   a 'I didn't really choose this life, but now I love it.'

   b 'I would love to do something different if I had the choice.'

   c 'I don't enjoy training, but I love performing.'

   d 'It's impossible to enjoy this way of life all the time.'

4 **For each question, complete the second sentence so that it means the same as the first. Use no more than three words.**

Tip: When you have written your answer, check that you have used no more than three words.

Example:

1 Mike phoned me a few second ago.

   Mike has _just phoned_ me.

2 Football is more exciting than tennis.

   Tennis isn't _____ football.

3 The water isn't warm enough to go swimming.

   The water _____ cold to go swimming.

4 We'll only go to watch the match if it's sunny.

   We won't go to watch the match _____ sunny.

5 We should book the tickets in advance.

   We _____ to book the tickets in advance.

6 It's not possible that's our hotel!

   That _____ our hotel!

5 **Your uncle has offered to buy you two tickets to a sports event for your birthday. Write a note to your friend Max. In your note, you should:**

• tell Max what the event is.

• explain why it will be exciting.

• invite Max to come to the event with you.

Write 35–45 words.

Tip: Count your words when you have finished. You mustn't write more than 45 words. Remember to include all the three points that are mentioned in the task.

6 **Read the exam task. Then look at questions a–f below, which will help you plan your story. Decide on the best order for the questions.**

> Your English teacher has asked you to write a story. This is the title for your story:
>
> My first time on stage
>
> Write your story in about 100 words.

   a ☐ What happened in the end?

   b ☐ How did you feel before you went on stage?

   c ☐ What happened next?

   d ☐ [1] When and where did your performance take place?

   e ☐ How did you feel afterwards?

   f ☐ What was the first thing that happened when you started performing?

7 **Complete the sentences with the words below.**

> audience   cast   character
> costume   ~~lights~~   performance

1 The _lights_ suddenly went out when I started to sing.

2 The _____ clapped loudly at the end of the show.

3 The other members of the _____ helped me.

4 My _____ didn't fit very well.

5 I was playing a very funny _____.

6 In the end, I gave a good _____.

8 **Write your answer to the exam task in Exercise 6.**

1 Read the text and choose the correct letter (a, b, c or d) for each space.

Tip: When you look at the four options for each gap, think about the meaning of each word. Also think about the words or grammar patterns it is usually used with. Then decide which option best fills the gap.

Crime *and* punishment

Societies have always found it difficult to ¹_____ with the problem of young criminals. In the past young people who ²_____ crimes were often sent to prison. Many judges believed that this was the best way to ³_____ them. They thought that if they didn't treat these youngsters severely, they ⁴_____ never change their ways. It is certainly true that if a young person ⁵_____ an old person, for example, they should pay a price for this action. But the question is whether the best solution is to send them to prison, ⁶_____ they will meet and ⁷_____ out with older, more experienced criminals.

Many experts now believe it is important to help young criminals to ⁸_____ changes to their life, rather than simply locking them away. They say it is better to help these young people to ⁹_____ new skills. This will help them to ¹⁰_____ a job in the future and hopefully stay away from crime. Of course, someone who has ¹¹_____ their house burgled by a young criminal may not agree with this gentle approach!

Example:

1 ⓐ deal	b solve	c get on	d fall out
2 a made	b committed	c did	d acted
3 a hurt	b catch	c punish	d arrest
4 a will	b can	c must	d would
5 a steals	b robs	c breaks	d damages
6 a where	b which	c who	d that
7 a chat	b discuss	c hang	d spend
8 a do	b get	c take	d make
9 a learn	b do	c revise	d memorise
10 a go	b get	c take	d win
11 a watched	b made	c suffered	d had

2 Look at the sentences about a TV show. Read the text to decide if each sentence is correct (C) or incorrect (I).

Tip: The sentences follow the same order as the text, but different words and expressions may be used in the sentences and the text.

1 ☐ Bethany learned about the TV show at school.

2 ☐ Bethany decided to apply after talking to Lou.

3 ☐ Bethany was disappointed because she didn't learn much on the interview day.

4 ☐ Bethany didn't expect to get onto the show because there was a limited number of places.

5 ☐ Staying quiet in classes was very difficult for Bethany.

6 ☐ In a Science lesson, Bethany learned about how people first landed on the moon.

7 ☐ Bethany didn't enjoy the 1950s homework, but she thinks it had some advantages.

8 ☐ It took Bethany longer than usual to write her essays.

9 ☐ Bethany loved the food in the 1950s school canteen.

10 ☐ Bethany thinks she will definitely continue to use the cooking skills she learned.

1950s School by Bethany Jones

Last year I saw an advert in a history magazine asking for young people to take part in a reality TV show called *1950s School*. The idea was to take a group of young people and transport them back to a 1950s school so they could experience what school life was like for teenagers at that time. At first, I wasn't particularly keen, but my friend Lou thought it was a great idea and she persuaded me to put my name forward.

To apply, we had to write about ourselves and why we were interested in the show, and then have an interview with the programme's director. The interview day was fun. They told us a lot about what our lives would be like for three months if we were accepted, although, unfortunately, we didn't get an opportunity to look round the school. I was really excited, but I didn't want to get my hopes up because there were loads of people there and I knew they only wanted fifteen. I was amazed a week later when I received a letter saying that they wanted me to take part.

I was surprised at how different the lessons were to our lessons nowadays. The teachers were all really strict, and in lessons we had to just listen and take notes and not talk at all. That was really hard for me because I love chatting! In Physics, we learned about space but not much was known at that time because this was ten years before people landed on the moon. And, of course, lessons like ICT didn't exist at all in the 1950s.

I found the homework quite boring. At my school we do a lot of projects, which I love. But at the 1950s school we had to just memorise a lot of facts. I really didn't enjoy that but actually, it's quite useful now because I can tell you all the capital cities of Europe! One of the hardest things was writing essays. I usually use my laptop for writing and I'm quite fast at typing, but it took me ages to write everything by hand.

One good thing was the school meals. I usually take sandwiches to eat at lunchtime, but in the 1950s all schools served hot meals at lunchtime. It was fun sitting eating with all the others in the canteen, although the food wasn't brilliant! The best part of the whole experience for me was the Cooking lessons. It was strange because only the girls learned Cooking, while the boys practised making things out of wood. But I loved learning how to make bread and cakes. That's one thing from the past that I'll definitely do more of in the future!

3 These people are all working on a project about their ideal school. Below are descriptions of eight schools. Decide which school (A–H) would be the most suitable for each person (1–5).

Tip: Each person mentions two or three important points. Some of these points may be mentioned in more than one description, but only one description matches all the points.

1 ☐ Abbie wants to get good exam results so she can go to university. She would prefer small classes, with extra help for subjects she finds difficult. She is especially interested in History and would like to go to a boarding school.

2 ☐ Frank is very sporty and enjoys being physically active. He does very well in a teamwork environment. He sometimes finds it difficult to concentrate if lessons are too long.

3 ☐ Louise is very creative and enjoys lessons such as art and drama. She learns best through doing things, rather than through studying with books. She would like opportunities to be involved in performances at school.

4 ☐ Jamie doesn't like memorising lots of facts. He's interested in learning how to think for himself and learning skills that will be useful to him in his future working life. He doesn't want to go to a boarding school.

5 ☐ Paula is interested in lots of different subjects and enjoys exploring topics in a lot of detail. She's confident and hard-working and enjoys working alone. She enjoys helping younger children to learn.

Schools

A Grange Hill School

At Grange Hill School we believe in a modern approach to education, and our focus is on learning to learn rather than just taking in facts. We therefore offer lessons in critical thinking skills and problem solving, as well as practical subjects such as ICT, which will enable our students to succeed once they leave school and start their careers.

B King Edwards Academy

At King Edwards Academy we know that our traditional teaching methods work because our students achieve excellent exam results. Students are taught in large classes and there are regular tests to check their progress. At the same time, many of our students are creative, so we offer a range of after-school clubs where students can enjoy music and art activities.

C Mill Street School

We believe that it's important to educate the mind and body at the same time. Our school day starts with exercise and lessons are kept short to allow frequent breaks for students. Students are encouraged to work in groups and discuss their learning. The school has excellent sports facilities and all students are encouraged to take part.

D Helpton High School

Our belief is that students work best when they're studying things they're interested in. Our timetable allows plenty of free time for students, when they can work independently on projects they have chosen themselves. Older students have the opportunity to work with teachers and provide support for students just starting at the school.

E Queen Anne's School

Our students get great results, and over ninety percent continue their studies when they leave school. Teaching is done in small groups and, because students live at the school during term time, there is plenty of time for them to meet teachers in the evening if they need extra help. There are frequent trips to museums and other places of interest.

F Paston School

Paston School is a small community school with a friendly atmosphere. We specialise in teaching practical skills such as cooking and gardening, along with all the traditional school subjects. We believe that students learn best if they are calm and happy, so every day starts with a yoga and relaxation class.

G Bridgeport Academy

At Bridgeport Academy we believe that imagination, rather than memorising facts, is the key to successful learning. Our students do a lot of practical work and we encourage them to express themselves and use their own ideas. The school has its own art gallery and an excellent Drama department.

H Elmswood School

Elmswood School is a specialist science and technology school. Although lessons are taught in all subjects, there is a special emphasis on Maths, Science subjects and ICT. We are a boarding school with accommodation for about 800 students. Many of our students go on to become successful scientists or engineers.

4 For each question, complete the second sentence so that it means the same as the first. Use no more than three words.

Tip: When you have written your answer, read both sentences again carefully to check that they have exactly the same meaning. Remember to check that you have used no more than three words.

Example:

1 Mike phoned me a few second ago.
   Mike has *just phoned* me.
2 I lived in this house when I was younger.
   This is the _____ lived when I was younger.
3 You should call the police immediately.
   If I were _____ call the police immediately.
4 The police caught the burglars.
   The burglars _____ the police.
5 Someone stole my bike yesterday.
   I had _____ yesterday.
6 Who was your piano teacher?
   Who _____ to play the piano?

5 You are going to take part in a cycle race, but your bike was stolen. Write a note to your friend Rob. In your note, you should:

- explain when and where your bike was stolen.
- ask to borrow Rob's bike.
- say when you will need it.

Write **35–45 words.**

Tip: Use informal language to make your note sound friendly. Remember to include all the three points that are mentioned and to count your words when you have finished.

6 Read the exam task. Then look at ideas a–h below about your best friend. Tick (✓) the five ideas that are relevant to the topic of the letter.

> This is part of a letter you receive from an English friend:
>
> I've just read a book about best friends. Tell me about your best friend. How long have you been friends and how did you meet? What interests do you share?
>
> Now write a letter answering your friend's questions.
> Write your letter in about 100 words.

a ☐ his/her life before I knew him/her
b ☑ where and when I first met him/her
c ☐ what we were doing when we first met
d ☐ his/her personality
e ☐ other members of his/her family
f ☐ his/her house or flat
g ☐ a hobby or activity that we both like
h ☐ why we get on well together

7 Complete sentences and phrases 1–6 with the words below. Then answer questions a–c.

> asked best ~~hear~~ soon
> thank wanted

1 It was good to *hear* from you.
2 You _____ to know about my best friend.
3 All the _____ ,
4 You _____ about my best friend.
5 See you _____ ,
6 _____ you for your letter.

Which two sentences/phrases:

a are used to start a letter? *1,* _____
b make it clear why you're writing?
   _____
c are used to end a letter? _____

8 Read the exam task. Then look at questions 1–6, which will help you plan your story. Complete the questions with the phrases below.

> did Tom do next the end
> the first thing ~~was Tom feeling~~
> when he arrived

> Your English teacher has asked you to write a story. Your story must begin with this sentence:
>
> Tom was feeling happy as he walked to school.
>
> Write your story in about 100 words.

1 Why *was Tom feeling* happy?
2 What was _____ that happened as he was walking along?
3 What _____ when this happened?
4 What happened _____ ?
5 What happened in
   _____ ?
6 How did Tom feel _____ at school?

9 Write your answer to one of the exam tasks in Exercises 6 and 8.

Unit 1

Exercise 1
1 charger 2 selfie stick 3 share
4 download 5 awful 6 perfect

Exercise 2
1 twice 2 useful 3 ugly 4 made
5 break 6 evening

Exercise 3
1 am chatting 2 don't often watch 3 lives
4 don't like 5 isn't raining 6 doesn't want

Exercise 4
1 Do you often read, don't 2 Is Jamie listening, is
3 Do you think, do 4 Are your friends making,
are 5 Are you doing, 'm not 6 Do your friends
always remember, don't

Exercise 5
1 being 2 to pay 3 to listen 4 to stay up
5 waiting 6 to go

Exercise 6
1 Shall 2 idea 3 could 4 sure 5 Why
6 not 7 what 8 not 9 Let

Unit 2

Exercise 1
1 sunny 2 wind 3 foggy 4 mild 5 freezing
6 degrees 7 flood 8 earthquake

Exercise 2
1 leaves 2 path 3 make 4 discovered
5 really 6 absolutely

Exercise 3
1 stayed 2 didn't see 3 went 4 took
5 didn't want 6 Did, have

Exercise 4
1 wasn't watching 2 was swimming
3 weren't chatting 4 Was the sun shining, was
5 Were the bears sleeping, weren't

Exercise 5
1 saw, was walking 2 were skiing, happened
3 watched, were staying 4 was sitting, got
5 were watching, when

Exercise 6
1 c 2 b 3 a 4 b

Exercise 7
1 Why did you do that? 2 I didn't realise
3 I didn't mean to 4 I really wanted
5 be more careful

Unit 3

Exercise 1
1 garlic 2 cream 3 nuts 4 cheese
5 honey 6 flour

Exercise 2
1 building 2 contestant 3 win 4 do
5 make 6 do 7 delicious 8 fresh

Exercise 3
1 hasn't started yet 2 Have you ever tried
3 have just finished 4 have never seen
5 Has it stopped raining yet

Exercise 4
1 c 2 b 3 a 4 c

Exercise 5
1 for 2 since 3 since 4 for

Exercise 6
1 have visited 2 didn't go 3 enjoyed
4 has opened 5 wrote, hasn't replied
6 have never had, tried

Exercise 7
1 Nearly 2 Could I have 3 Of course
4 Would you like 5 Thank you

Unit 4

Exercise 1
1 sci-fi 2 cartoon 3 performance
4 character 5 hit 6 audience

Exercise 2
1 vacation 2 toilet 3 dance 4 life
5 party 6 cake

Exercise 3
1 more popular than 2 were too
3 the tallest 4 as expensive as
5 the best play 6 old enough to

Exercise 4
1 many 2 lots of 3 any 4 much
5 few 6 little

Exercise 5
1 well 2 early 3 quietly 4 angrily
5 fast 6 late

Exercise 6
1 I'd rather 2 it sounds 3 Where would you
rather 4 I'd prefer 5 Which would you prefer
6 very scary

Unit 5

Exercise 1
1 basketball 2 diving 3 snowboarding
4 yoga 5 ice-skating 6 climbing

Exercise 2
1 pitch 2 kit 3 fans 4 score 5 do
6 have 7 player 8 practise 9 take

Exercise 3
1 opens 2 'll win 3 's going to score
4 'm going to take up 5 'm meeting
6 'll pay

Exercise 4
1 'll get, take up 2 don't practise, won't get
3 won't win, run 4 rains, 'll play 5 'll arrive, is

Exercise 5
1 S 2 D 3 D 4 S

Exercise 6
1 up to 2 Nothing much 3 What about
4 don't know 5 got any plans 6 First
7 Then 8 your plans

Unit 6

Exercise 1
1 platform 2 ticket 3 trip 4 cruise 5 break
6 camp

Exercise 2
1 reservation 2 view 3 double 4 sunglasses
5 torch 6 guidebook 7 journey 8 travel

Exercise 3
1 f 2 i 3 b 4 c 5 e 6 h

Exercise 4
1 a 2 b 3 a 4 b 5 b 6 a

Exercise 5
1 didn't catch, What I asked 2 first part, I said
that 3 say that again, just saying

Unit 7

Exercise 1
1 b 2 f 3 c 4 e 5 a 6 d

Exercise 2
1 hang 2 out 3 put 4 sense 5 having 6 in
7 got 8 has

Exercise 3
1 spent, would get 2 would go, was/were 3 had, would
travel 4 would talk, were 5 would do, lived

Exercise 4
1 who 2 where 3 who 4 which 5 that 6 where

Exercise 5
1 grandmother, who is seventy-six, is still very
2 uncle, who is a doctor, works at the main hospital
3 , where my cousins live, is on the
4 bike, which he got for his birthday, is really
5 suggested going to the pizza restaurant in town, where
they do

Exercise 6
1 up to 2 a laugh 3 Who's that boy 4 do you mean
5 tall one 6 at the back 7 She's wearing

Unit 8

Exercise 1
1 shoplifter 2 fine 3 jail 4 vandal 5 theft 6 judge

Exercise 2
1 climbed 2 robbing 3 committed 4 chased
5 broke 6 escape

Exercise 3
1 solve 2 fingerprints 3 arrest 4 witness
5 clue 6 suspect

Exercise 4
1 are used 2 was arrested 3 was found 4 is solved

Exercise 5
1 We need to get our TV repaired. 2 I had my bike stolen.
3 Shall we get a pizza delivered? 4 He's having a new
suit made.

Exercise 6
2 incorrect 3 impossible 4 unusual

Exercise 7
1 don't know 2 fine 3 try 4 OK 5 worry
6 suppose 7 sure

Unit 9

Exercise 1
1 Maths 2 practical exam 3 ICT 4 performance
5 Literature 6 project

Exercise 2
1 revise 2 memorise 3 learning 4 lazy
5 take 6 fill in

Exercise 3
1 problem 2 teamwork 3 general 4 critical
5 mistakes 6 mess

Exercise 4
1 Do your friends go 2 Have you finished
3 Why is Carrie 4 Who called 5 Who did you see

Exercise 5
a 3 b 5 c 2 d 1 e 4

Exercise 6
1 I play 2 stole 3 were walking 4 has become
5 will help 6 starts

Exercise 7
1 How have 2 Do you like 3 How was
4 Have you been 5 What are 6 Would you like